100

THINGS TO DO IN
TUSCALOOSA
BEFORE YOU
DIE

100
THINGS TO DO IN
TUSCALOOSA
BEFORE YOU
DIE

• •

BECKY BEALL

REEDY PRESS

Library of Congress Control Number: 2024930392

ISBN: 9781681064734

Design by Jill Halpin

Printed in the United States of America
24 25 26 27 28   5 4 3 2 1

We (the publisher and the author) have done our best to provide the most accurate information available when this book was completed. However, we make no warranty, guarantee, or promise about the accuracy, completeness, or currency of the information provided, and we expressly disclaim all warranties, express or implied. Please note that attractions, company names, addresses, websites, and phone numbers are subject to change or closure, and this is outside of our control. We are not responsible for any loss, damage, injury, or inconvenience that may occur due to the use of this book. When exploring new destinations, please do your homework before you go. You are responsible for your own safety and health when using this book.

DEDICATION

To Larry, my biggest cheerleader and toughest critic,
forever travel companion, best friend, and love of my life.
Sharing a passion for Alabama football and a love for
Tuscaloosa has brought us to this moment.

To my kiddos—the fabulous four—Meaghan (Barry), Chelsea,
Taylor (Colton), and Eli, who daily encourage me to be better.

To my grands, who are the absolute light of my life.

To friends, family, and all who hold this Southern
college town close—Roll Tide!

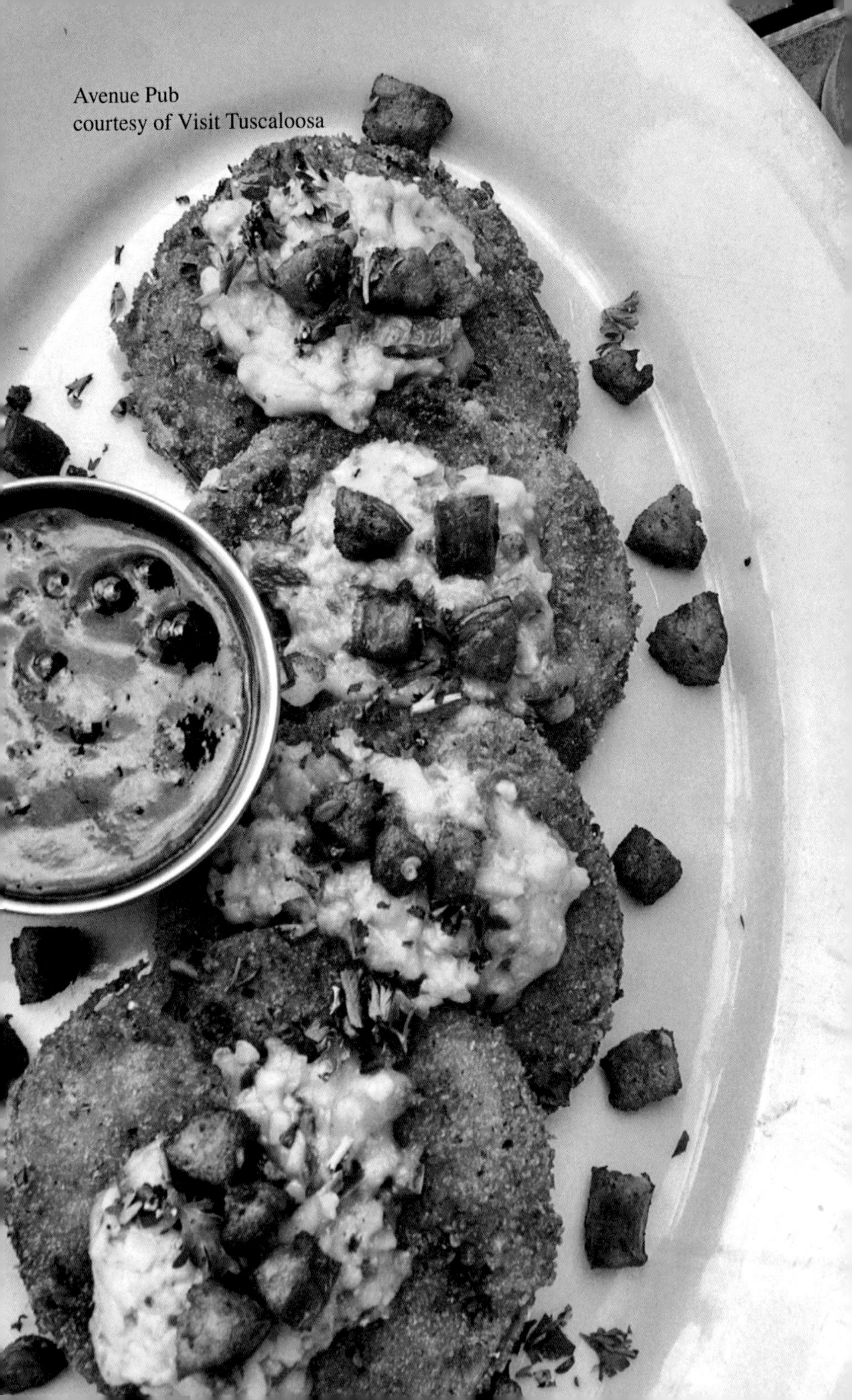

Avenue Pub
courtesy of Visit Tuscaloosa

CONTENTS

• •

Sports and Recreation

• •

Culture and History

● ●

Shopping and Fashion

• •

ACKNOWLEDGMENTS

Many thanks to all who offered suggestions and encouragement during the writing of this book. Much like raising a family, it takes a village, and I'm thankful that my village is large! From writer friends who answered questions to family who pushed me to the finish line, you all are appreciated! Also, I would be remiss if I didn't mention the wonderful tourism professionals at Visit Tuscaloosa who were always ready for my next question or request. Finally, many heartfelt thanks to my dear friend Connie Nolen for many hours of discussion, and to her husband Jerry for the gorgeous photo used on the cover behind the "100."

Bama Elephant

PREFACE

Located along the Black Warrior River, Tuscaloosa is a special place to many. A former capital city, it has always stood out from neighboring small towns in West Alabama thanks to the University of Alabama. The campus and city are steeped in history with a heavy dose of college football fanfare. It's a place where "Roll Tide" is not only a battle cry but also a greeting.

A new generation calls Tuscaloosa home each year, but honored traditions create reasons for folks to come back again and again. Many first-time visitors come to enjoy a football game but immerse themselves in this community where art, museums, culture, scrumptious food, and outdoor activities are in no short supply. Tourists find value past their original travel purpose and a love affair is born.

Today's Tuscaloosa offers a taste of nostalgia mixed with Southern hospitality, along with amazing opportunities to experience one of Alabama's truest treasures. And, as a writer, it is my distinct pleasure to share 100 things in Tuscaloosa that will help jump-start your own memory-making excursions. From the walkable downtown district where entertainment flows to Bryant-Denny Stadium where the Tide rolls, Tuscaloosa is poised to share a legendary experience with you.

Urban Bar & Kitchen

FOOD
AND DRINK

SCORE BIG WITH CHICKEN WINGS AND MORE

AT BAUMHOWER'S VICTORY GRILLE

Baumhower's Victory Grille was the brainchild of Bob Baumhower, the All-American football legend from the University of Alabama and six-time All-Pro for the Miami Dolphins. In 1981, Baumhower began sharing his love for food by bringing Buffalo-style chicken wings to Alabama. Baumhower's college stomping grounds proved to be the perfect place to open his first restaurant, and now there are two locations in Tuscaloosa with several more across the state. Of course, legendary wings are the showstoppers, but they're far from the only thing on the menu. Enjoy watching sporting events on a myriad of televisions scattered throughout the restaurant while noshing on crowd-pleasers the likes of homemade fried mozzarella or Bam Bam Shrimp. Entrée choices range from salads and sandwiches to gourmet burgers, chicken, fish, and loads of sides. There's also a drink menu with lots of options from draft beers to craft cocktails.

500 Harper Lee Dr., 205-409-9922, (original location)
4251 Courtney Dr., 205-556-5658
baumhowers.com

FUN FACT

Baumhower's Victory Grille (original location) is home to the *Hey Coach* radio show on Thursday nights (6:30 to 8 p.m.) during football season beginning with the Thursday a week before the first game. While the restaurant is open to the public, you will need to have a seat reserved for the show audience if you plan to attend that particular event. You can only make that reservation in person, and a line forms well before 10 a.m. the day of. No reservations are accepted over the phone.

REVEL IN NOSTALGIA
AT THE HISTORIC WAYSIDER RESTAURANT

History runs deep at the Historic Waysider Restaurant where players, coaches, fans, locals, and tourists come to enjoy a true Southern breakfast or a meat-and-three lunch. The little red-and-white house not only serves the best biscuits in town, but it also pays homage to their favorite football team with vintage relics and memorabilia plastering the walls. Breakfast and lunch are the only two meals served at Waysider, except for the weekend when it's breakfast only. Will there be a line? Highly likely with only 16 tables, especially on weekends. Customer breakfast favorites include steak and eggs, pancakes, bacon, sausage, and their famous biscuits along with all the hot coffee you can drink. If it's a game-day weekend, kids get their pancakes shaped like elephants. Go figure! Lunch is only available on weekdays and offers down-home helpings of meat-and-threes.

1512 Greensboro Ave., 205-345-8239
facebook.com/thewaysider

TIP
Legendary Alabama football coach Paul "Bear" Bryant loved Waysider and could often be found sitting at a corner table eating some country ham. Today that table bears a bust of the coach with his iconic houndstooth fedora. Look for it!

DINE WITH THE LOCALS
AT NICK'S IN THE STICKS

Family-owned since 1953, Nick's in the Sticks is known for fantastic steaks, onion rings, a signature drink (the Nicodemus) and a laid-back atmosphere. Service in this small but lively establishment is stellar, and price tags make you forget about inflation. You're likely to have a wait, but quick service keeps things moving along. Want to be like the cool kids? Order a six- or eight-ounce. bacon-wrapped filet with an appetizer like chicken livers or fried shrimp. Not a steak fan? Try a burger, chicken, or catfish. Each entrée comes with a salad and choice of side (fries, onion rings, or baked potato) and a basket of bread for the table. There is also a kids' menu with yummy options like grilled cheese, fried shrimp, and chicken nuggets. Leave your mark at Nick's by adding a signed dollar bill to the ceiling collection. That's just how they roll in these parts.

4018 Culver Rd., 205-758-9316
nicks-in-the-sticks.com

NOSH ON FRENCH-INSPIRED FOODS
AT FORTÉ CUTS & COCKTAILS

Executive Chef Jacob Stull and his extraordinary cooking style have elevated the Tuscaloosa dining scene via Alamite Hotel's amazing foodie destination, Forté Cuts & Cocktails. Chef Stull has a phenomenal culinary background including time working as Chef de Partie at New Orleans famed Brennan's restaurant. Perfect for a fancy evening out or to celebrate a special occasion, Forté features French favorites and classic cuts along with a lovely bar and wine list, as well as seasonal delights. Start your meal with a nice cheese board or warm cheese pastry puffs, toss in an heirloom tomato salad, and complete it with an over-the-top entrée such as steak au poivre, beef bourguignon, a dry-aged rib eye, or filet mignon. Everything is fresh and plated beautifully. Reservations are preferred and may be arranged online for convenience.

2321 6th St., 205-794-8260
fortetcl.com

TIP

The Alamite, a boutique hotel property, is a
Marriott Tribute Portfolio hotel backed by a
group of partners that includes Alabama football
coach Nick Saban and his wife, Terry. If you are
looking to spend the night or a few days, this is
a lovely choice with 112 upscale rooms in the
downtown area just minutes from Bryant-Denny
Stadium and the Mercedes-Benz Amphitheater.

Alamite Hotel Tuscaloosa
2301 6th St., 205-860-7998
thealamite.com

EAT YOUR VEGGIES
AT CITY CAFE

City Cafe in nearby Northport packs the place daily serving meals even a college kid can afford. Open Monday through Friday for breakfast and lunch, the restaurant offers tried-and-true, stick-to-your-ribs dishes. Breakfast starts at 4 a.m. offering biscuits stuffed with whatever you like (bologna, sausage, bacon, ham, eggs, or cheese) or just plain. Add a side of grits, oatmeal, or toast for a complete meal. Need a little more? Choose a larger meal like pancakes, sausage and biscuits, or an omelet. The lunch menu is sorted by the days of the week and packed with Southern meat-and-threes. Find your favorites among the ranks of chicken, roast beef, meat loaf, catfish, hamburger steak, and loads of vegetables like peas, beans, corn, mashed potatoes, turnip greens, and many more. Best of all, you can order cobbler in place of one of your veggies. Now, that's special!

408 Main Ave., Northport, 205-758-9171
facebook.com/citycafenorthportal

UNLEASH YOUR APPETITE
AT SOUTHERN ALE HOUSE

Known for Southern cuisine and upscale and unique bar food, Southern Ale House is anything but ordinary. Everyday dishes are screaming with exciting twists and turns, taking hamburgers to extraordinary new heights (case in point, the Pimento Jalapeño Cream Cheese Burger). Meanwhile, menu offerings continue to cast appeal to every diner with exceptional choices such as Blackened Redfish with Crawfish Cream Sauce over Roasted Creole Rice Pilaf. With a diverse opportunity to serve more than just salads, sandwiches, and desserts, this is a restaurant you can come to as a solo diner or bring the family. There are lots of beers on tap, and flights are available. Craft cocktails are as scrumptious as they are pretty (think Pineapple Express or Blueberry Lemon Drop), so prepare to delight your taste buds! Don't miss a chance to dine on the patio, where there's often live music.

1530 McFarland Blvd. N, 205-248-7500
southernalehouse.com

FUEL UP FOR YOUR DAY
AT HERITAGE HOUSE COFFEE AND TEA

College town must-haves include caffeine sources for all-day cram sessions as well as fuel for visitors in town for football fanfare and beyond. Heritage House was Tuscaloosa's first official coffee shop, opening in 1993, and today, the third owner, Rebekah Wanstall, has done remarkable things. Offering a sweet pastry case brimming with baked-from-scratch goodies, plus café-style lunches, dozens of coffees sourced worldwide, fantastic teas, and a great place to hang out with friends, Wanstall continues to serve out her purpose for Heritage House to be a refuge of peace in the midst of a broken world. While Heritage House has grown to three locations, each with its own vibe, good service is constant across them all. Nods to humble beginnings and traditions of yesteryear remain steadfast through mismatched chairs, furnishings, and table settings. As eclectic as it may be, it radiates Southern charm. Come sip here!

2370 Jack Warner Pkwy., 205-562-9135
700 Towncenter Blvd., 205-758-0042, (original location)
5600 Rice Mine Rd. NE, 205-737-7720
heritagehousecoffee.com

COFFEE OR TEA, IF YOU PLEASE

Babe's Doughnut + Coffee
500 Greensboro Ave., 205-722-2154
facebook.com/babestuscaloosa

BobaMania
Premium Bubble Tea
1914 University Blvd., 205-227-8805
1800 McFarland Blvd. E, Ste. 434, 659-243-9273
bobamania.com

Just Love Coffee Cafe
2531 University Blvd., Ste. 100, 205-759-2587
justlovecoffeecafe.com

Monarch Espresso Bar
714 22nd Ave., 205-210-8751
monarchespresso.com

Pastor's Coffee
2507 McFarland Blvd., Northport, 205-330-2515
pastorskitchennorthport.com/coffee

Strange Brew Coffeehouse
1101 University Blvd., 205-469-7250
facebook.com/strangebrewbam

Turbo Coffee
2010 8th St., 205-860-5117
turbocoffee.co

FEAST ON MOUTHWATERING RIBS
AT DREAMLAND BBQ

Folks in these parts will vouch for Dreamland ribs any day of the week. They're as iconic in Tuscaloosa as national championships, and it is imperative that you eat a meal at this barbecue joint when in town. John "Big Daddy" Bishop went from dream to restaurant when he opened Dreamland BBQ in 1958. Hickory-fired ribs, white bread, and a lip-smacking "special" sauce brought barbecue lovers from all over to dine with Bishop. Today, more than six decades later, pitmasters continue to prepare spareribs over a hickory wood-fired pit, basting them with their signature sauce. The menu today includes chicken, smoked sausage, a handful of sides, and a couple of desserts. Banana pudding is a no-brainer in the South, and your souvenir should be a jar of their sauce. If you are struggling between entrées, remember the tagline that started it all: "Ain't nothing like 'em nowhere." Get the ribs.

5535 15th Ave. E, 205-758-8135
dreamlandbbq.com/locations/tuscaloosa

101 Bridge Ave., Northport, 205-343-6677
dreamlandbbq.com/locations/northport

MORE SAUCY CHOICES

Archibald & Woodrow's BBQ
4215 Greensboro Ave., 205-331-4858
archibaldbbq.com

Full Moon Bar-B-Que
1434 McFarland Blvd. E, 205-366-3555
fullmoonbbq.com/locations/tuscaloosa

Jim 'N Nick's
305 21st Ave., 205-469-2060
jimnnicks.com/locations/al/tuscaloosa

Moe's Original BBQ
2101 University Blvd., 205-752-3616
moesoriginalbbq.com/lo/tuscaloosa

Thomas Rib Shack
2931 15th St., 205-759-5010
thomasribsshack.com

DAZZLE YOUR TASTE BUDS
AT DILLARD'S CHOPHOUSE

Dillard's Chophouse is an excellent dining choice with a robust menu complemented by amazing service. Featured entrées include house-made pastas, hand-cut steaks, surf and turf, and other signature specials, but don't overlook starters like jumbo lump crab cakes or New Orleans BBQ shrimp. These appetizers could easily be paired with a salad and a side for a complete meal. As fine-dining steakhouses go, Dillard's has some killer steak cuts, including 8-, 10-, and 12-ounce filet mignons; a 22-ounce cowboy cut; and others you might fancy from the New York Strip or Delmonico variety. Pair any of these with scallops, shrimp, or a lobster tail for an over-the-top surf and turf. The sides are all delectable, but the lobster macaroni and cheese is to die for! Reservations are encouraged and can be made online.

2330 4th St., 205-614-8782
dillardschophouse.com

TIP
Cruise the list of available vinos given the *Wine Spectator* Award of Excellence Dillard's has tucked away in their back pocket. That's a good sign that they'll have good wine.

ENJOY THE PATIO
AT AVENUE PUB

Things people love about Avenue Pub start with a convenient downtown location and end with food and drink favorites. This casual restaurant offers a family-friendly atmosphere with a nice patio for those who love being outdoors. Commitments like making in-house menu items fresh, serving Alabama beers, and providing local entertainment are all testaments to a standard of excellence that Avenue Pub continues to strive for. Open for brunch, lunch, and dinner, you'll find foods you recognize (and crave) like sandwiches, salads, burgers, fish and chips, and (on the dinner menu) salmon filet. All meals are beautifully plated, looking too good to eat . . . almost! Follow their Facebook page to track day-to-day offerings like trivia nights, Tequila Tuesday, Whiskey Wednesday specials, and live music days. There's always something entertaining at Avenue Pub. Grab a Loretta Lemonade or a Honeybee and see for yourself.

2230 University Blvd., 205-759-4900
avepub.com

TIP
Visit Avenue Pub Upstairs for beer and libations, plus an abbreviated menu.

LIVE YOUR
FOODIE DREAM
AT RIVER

When in the mood for an exceptional dining experience, think of River, where they deliver the whole package from ambiance to service to food. Location is key, and views from the banks of the Black Warrior River just can't be beat. Choose terrace seating, order a signature cocktail like an Orange Dreamsickle or a Bombay Basil Refresher, and get ready to make all your foodie dreams come true. Serving brunch, lunch, and dinner, you can count on impressive options for all three meals. With a chef-driven menu that won't disappoint, starters (shareables) are a beautiful beginning to any meal. A fresh farm salad, sausage board, or pork belly are excellent first courses and complement other menu items like rib eyes and filets, chicken, pasta, and seasonal fish. If you can find room for dessert, the house-made crème brûlée or oatmeal cream pie are two popular ways to end your meal. You can always share, right?

1650 Jack Warner Pkwy., Ste. 1005, 205-632-3801
rivertuscaloosa.com

TIP

Want to try River drinks and cocktails at a discount? Check out Happy Hour 4:30 to 6:30 p.m. on Tuesday and Thursday and all night on Wednesday. Choose from $5 select wines, draft beer, well drinks, and bubble cocktails, or $7 for the nightly special cocktail.

FILL YOUR PLATE (AND BELLY)
AT FIVE BAR

Five Bar has got it going on with a unique twist on menus and a following that's as loyal as Alabama football fans. On weekdays, Five serves lunch and dinner with weekends reserved for brunch and dinner. Each menu offers "The Five," which are entrée choices, but there will also be some snack (appetizer) choices and five signature cocktails, five domestic beers, five craft beers, plus five each of red and white wines. Menus are filled with excellent options like a double cheeseburger, gulf sandwich and fries, or even red beans and rice. Brunch is a weekend favorite with comfort foods such as chicken and waffles, shrimp 'n' grits, steak and hash, a breakfast cheeseburger, and the Five burrito. Toss in a Bloody Mary bar, mimosas with fresh-squeezed OJ, and caramel-apple beignets for bonus points!

2324 6th St., 205-345-6089
five-bar.com/location/tuscaloosa-alabama

TIP
Don't overlook Five Java located right next to Five Bar. It's a coffee and juice bar with breakfast foods, pastries, and lunch. There's café-style seating, or take it outdoors when the weather is behaving.

DROP IN
FOR WINGS AND BURGERS
AT BUFFALO PHIL'S

Buffalo Phil's is a hoppin' spot on the strip, especially when the Tide has a home game. It's only a couple of blocks from the stadium, right on the strip, and has a patio for outdoor seating. Those who frequent Phil's will recommend ordering wings, their specialty, smothered in Phil's original recipe plus a great selection of sauces in amazing flavors (honey BBQ, teriyaki, and crimson, to name a few). Other menu offerings range from salads, sandwiches and chicken fingers to delicious burgers like the all-new Bama Jam Burger served on Texas toast with cream cheese, jalapeños, bacon, and habanero bacon jam. No matter what you order, get your party started with some mac 'n' cheese bites or some fried pickles (a Southern delicacy). There's beer, wine, specialty drinks, and shots, but consider tasting Phil's signature drink, the Philibuster, that comes in a souvenir cup!

1149 University Blvd., 205-758-3318
buffalophils.com

TIP

Buffalo Phil's has nice lunch specials Monday through Friday from 11 a.m. to 3 p.m. including the Bama Jam Burger, wing selections, and the grown-up grilled cheese. Same great taste for a little less money.

PARTAKE IN PASTA
AT DEPALMA'S ITALIAN CAFE

DePalma's has been serving the Tuscaloosa area since 1995 with a taste of Italy in one of the area's most beautiful historic buildings that just so happens to have some Italian architectural vibes. Built in 1892, the Richardsonian Romanesque-style building has been used for a few different businesses over the years. It's easy to spot on the corner of University Boulevard and 23rd Avenue, with its stately appearance and striped awning.

Dining at DePalma's is a pleasure, with a myriad of choices from appetizers and breadsticks to calzones, pasta dishes, and specialties, all made with the freshest of ingredients. Locals swear by the white chocolate bread pudding, but DePalma's also serves wonderful tiramisu and cannolis. Additionally, the wine list is extensive and available by the glass or bottle. The atmosphere is family friendly, so stop in and have a true Italian dining experience that you won't soon forget.

2300 University Blvd., 205-759-1879
depalmasdowntown.com

TEMPT YOUR TASTE BUDS
WITH THE BEST PIZZAS IN TOWN

Blaze Pizza
1800 McFarland Blvd. E, 205-764-5848
locations.blazepizza.com/alabama/tuscaloosa

Broadway Pizzaria North
4550 Station Cir., Northport, 205-330-6969

Broadway Pizzeria South
5400 McFarland Blvd. E, 205-722-1047
broadwaypizzeria.net

Heat Pizza Bar
2250 6th St., 205-632-3282
heatpizzabar.com

Mr. G's Italian Restaurant
908 McFarland Blvd., Northport, 205-339-8505
mrgstuscaloosa.com

Pyro's Fire Fresh Pizza
1320 McFarland Blvd. E, 205-248-7343
pyrospizza.com

The Standard
1217 University Blvd., 205-247-9876
thestandardbama.com

ENJOY
A ROMANTIC DINNER
AT EVANGELINE'S

When the evening calls for intimate dining at its best, head to Evangeline's and soak in the romantic ambiance in addition to a fabulous menu of flavorful, over-the-top dishes. Note that the menu is seasonal, so it will change throughout the year. However, no matter the season, your plate will be brimming with fresh, high-quality foods plated to impress. Beginnings (starters) are great plays on chicken, shrimp, crab cakes, and flatbreads. Salads are absolutely fabulous, and it's perfectly acceptable to add a protein to create an entrée. The main courses are stunners… their own seafood masterpieces, Angus beef selections, and usually a chicken and/or pasta as well. It's hard to imagine that this wouldn't quickly become every couple's favorite Tuscaloosa dining spot. Keep in mind they are only open Tuesday through Saturday from 5 to 9 p.m. It's best to make a reservation online.

1653 McFarland Blvd. N, 205-752-0830
evangelinestuscaloosa.com

GATHER AROUND THE TABLE
AT THE BLUE PLATE RESTAURANT

Since 2004, Blue Plate has been charming customers with traditional Southern foods that encourage gathering around the table for a meal. Order from a myriad of menu items that include soups, salads, and sandwiches, or order like the locals with a Blue Plate Special (an entrée and two sides). Good luck making a decision with chicken and dressing, catfish, pork roast, meat loaf, and country fried steak among the contenders. Veggies are no less plentiful, with choices that are tried-and-true Southern favorites featuring a variety of beans, peas, potatoes, corn, and many more. Also available are vegetable plates and a sampler plate, perfect for the indecisive diner who wants a small taste of several vegetables. Check out the dessert of the day; it'll be worth it. Come sit a spell. Catch up with friends and family. Enjoy food prepared in the spirit of Southern goodness.

450 McFarland Blvd., Northport, 205-462-3626
blueplaterestaurant.com

TASTE NEW ORLEANS
AT HALF SHELL OYSTER HOUSE

Partners of the Half Shell Oyster House brand started with one mission: to serve original New Orleans–inspired dishes with Southern hospitality in a distinct and vibrant French Quarter atmosphere. This single mission is evident in every aspect of your dining experience, from the building, the decor, the subtle sound of jazz music, the service, and, most of all, the food.

The menu is seasonal and offers a plethora of opportunities for the perfect Big Easy–style meal. Guests can pick from oysters (any way you like them), seafood, fish, steak, chicken, and pasta. Salads can be meals of their own by choosing to upgrade to an entrée portion. Then, there are handhelds like the voodoo chicken sandwich. It's hard to get more New Orleans than that.

This is not the place to skip dessert, as the offerings, though seasonal, are always superb. Cinnamon roll bread pudding is often a choice with its lovely spiced rum sauce. Sharing dessert is a worthy possibility, as is boxing it for later. No matter what you order, you can count on remarkable quality and the best in service. Those are nonnegotiables at Half Shell.

2325 University Blvd., 205-860-7001
halfshelloysterhouse.com/tuscaloosa

TIP

Half Shell Oyster House offers "just right" lunch portions at a "just right" price Monday through Friday from 11 a.m. to 3 p.m. Most are served with the choice of a side or salad, except for combos. This is a great way to get acquainted with their menu and save a few bucks.

SLIDE INTO SOUTHERN HOSPITALITY
AT SIDE BY SIDE
KITCHEN & COCKTAILS

Side by Side is aptly named because of its adjacency to the Embassy Suites hotel in downtown Tuscaloosa. Aside from that, one of the developers, Kem Wilson, had the idea while hunting. An heirloom side-by-side shotgun commonly used for duck hunting and often passed from generation to generation sparked a thought with Wilson, resonating with the way investing and managing hotels had been passed down in the family. Side by Side just seemed to fit. The cuisine is noted to be Southern comfort with a Creole twist using fresh ingredients from local artisan farms. Definitely a play on current farm-to-table trends. Try something different from this menu laden with scrumptious salads, and other dishes you just don't find every day (like Coffee Crusted Beef Tenderloin, Roll Tide Shrimp, or Herb Spatchcock Chicken). If you're a fan of after-dinner drinks, order a Southern Pecan Old Fashioned. You can thank me later.

2410 University Blvd., 205-561-5500
sidebysidekitchen.com

MEET YOUR FRIENDS
AT BROWN'S CORNER

The choices are many when it comes to date nights or meeting friends around town, but Brown's Corner is the coolest new place to dine, and it's right on University Boulevard. It's just upstairs from Half Shell Oyster House in a renovated space boasting the best of speakeasy-like elements along with a lounge. Cozy up with a classic cocktail and enjoy a fabulous dinner of lobster rolls, pasta, burgers, chicken, or a USDA choice filet. The sides are scrumptious and include a 3 Cheese Mac—Gouda, Gruyère, and American. You can't go wrong, right? The name may offer a nod to Brown's corner store from days gone by, but the present-day ambiance resonates with a carefully curated dining experience in a gorgeous, regal building. It seems more fitting to label such as a destination. One you'll want to visit again and again.

2325 University Blvd., top floor of Half Shell Oyster House, 205-860-7001
brownscornertuscaloosa.com

BITE INTO PERFECT CATFISH AND WINGS
AT CATFISH HEAVEN

Minutes from the University of Alabama campus, in the historic West End district of Tuscaloosa, a dream was born. In was March of 1993, and three young men launched a catfish restaurant dubbed Catfish Heaven. Two years later, the business was struggling, and one partner sold his interest back to the other two (who were brothers). The two brothers made a decision to add hot wings to the menu and became an overnight sensation. People loved them! Today Andrew and Wayne Robertson are living their dream and along the way have perfected their seasonings. They offer 10 wing flavors, catfish, whiting fish, coleslaw, fries, hush puppies, and a few desserts. You can dine in or order for carryout. It's strange, but most agree; the name says "catfish," but wings are the real show.

2502 21st St., 205-752-7222
catfishheaventuscaloosa.com

EXPERIENCE SIMPLE PLEASURES
AT URBAN BAR & KITCHEN

Dining options on University Boulevard run the gamut from bars and fast food to upscale restaurants. One that stands out with a minimalist interior, yet excellent service, and delicious food, plated oh so pretty, is Urban Bar & Kitchen. Attention to customer service has proven paramount to the success of this restaurant where simple decor lightly dresses the walls, leaving the food to be the center of attention. A nice selection of drinks along with a carefully curated menu creates a lovely experience that's easy to be a part of. The strawberry salad is affordable, beautiful, and scrumptious. Pair it with an appetizer like pulled pork nachos and you have a host of complementing flavors that are sure to please. There are also burgers, sandwiches, tacos, tastes from the sea, and nice sides to choose from. Quickly you'll learn that the lighted sign on the wall is truly accurate: this must be the place.

2321 University Blvd., 205-248-7162
urbanbarandkitchen.com

MAKE CRIMSON-COLORED MEMORIES
AT RAMA JAMA'S

Have you really been to Tuscaloosa if you haven't eaten at Rama Jama's? People pack in this establishment close to Bryant-Denny Stadium for the atmosphere, burgers, sweet tea, and milkshakes, but yes, they also have plenty of libations. Eat inside or outside; it's your choice. Either way, you'll be surrounded by crimson decor and lots of "Roll Tide" greetings!

Rama Jama's offers breakfast all day long, and sandwiches include a Southern favorite—bologna! If you need just a little more, ask for a 'Loosa steak and a fried pie. Souvenir cups are plentiful and double as glassware in most T-Town dorms. Be sure to snap an Instagram-worthy selfie during your visit to document your time at Rama Jama's making crimson-colored memories. You'll feel like a local in no time at all!

1000 Paul W Bryant Dr., 205-737-7524
instagram.com/rama_jamas

SATISFY YOUR SWEET TOOTH

Alley Cake Co.
412 22nd Ave., Northport, 205-345-8610

Edgar's Bakery
1653 McFarland Blvd. N, 205-987-0790
edgarsbakery.com

Insomnia Cookies
1130 University Blvd., 205-509-1565
insomniacookies.com

Mi Casita Mexican Bakery
513 Hargrove E Rd., 256-945-5160

Moonshot Creamery + Bottle Shop
1650 Jack Warner Pkwy., Ste. 1008, 205-210-8751
moonshotcreamery.com

The Peach Cobbler Factory
1130 University Blvd., Ste. B-4, 205-737-7474
peachcobblerfactory.com

The Biscuit Shop Co.
80 McFarland Blvd., Northport, 662-324-3118
thebiscuitlady.com

HANG OUT
AT THE HOUNDSTOOTH SPORTS BAR

The Houndstooth Sports Bar, named for the beloved fedora worn by former University of Alabama football coach Paul "Bear" Bryant, sits only two blocks from Bryant-Denny Stadium. Alabama's favorite college bar beckons visitors and locals alike to come in for the coldest beer in town, tons of state-of-the-art TVs, pool tables, dartboards, and events that go on long past football season. The Houndstooth has amassed quite a string of accolades including "#1 College Sports Bar" by *Sports Illustrated on Campus*, "Best College Sports Bar" by *Playboy* magazine, "Top 50 Southern Bars" by *Garden & Gun* magazine, and "One of America's Best College Bars" by *Travel + Leisure* magazine. Locals are proud of these accolades. Visitors want to be a part of it. Come hang out on the patio, grab a drink, and cheer on the Tide!

1300 University Blvd., 205-752-8444
houndstoothsportsbar.com

CATCH A GOOD TIME BARHOPPING

Catch 22
Known for the best infused drinks
2328 6th St., 205-344-9347
facebook.com/catch22bar

Gallettes
Home to the Yellow Hammer drink
1021 University Blvd., 205-792-3961
instagram.com/uagallettes

Harry's Bar
Tuscaloosa's oldest drinking establishment (1972)
1330 Hargrove Rd., 205-758-9332
facebook.com/harrysttown

Innisfree Irish Pub
1925 University Blvd., 205-345-1199
innisfreeirishpubs.com

The Gray Lady
521 Greensboro Ave., 205-469-9521
facebook.com/grayladyttown

The Red Shed
509 Red Drew Ave., 205-248-2116
facebook.com/theredshedtuscaloosa

Top Shelf Tavern
407 23rd Ave., 205-343-0020
topshelftuscaloosa.com

ROLL INTO DINNER
AT AJIAN SUSHI

Former Alabama quarterback A. J. McCarron left his mark on the football field, and now his imprint is on the city of Tuscaloosa as well. McCarron opened a trendy sushi restaurant, Ajian Sushi, near downtown, offering a one-of-a-kind signature sushi roll fit for a champion. Sushi lovers can celebrate their beloved team with food choices like the Maki Tide roll. The simplicity of the atmosphere and menu options at Ajian are direct reflections of the Japanese term "shibui," referring to an aesthetic of simple, subtle, and unobtrusive beauty. It's perfect for Ajian, a healthy dining option where you pick the rice, wrap, fresh ingredients, sauces, and toppings. The build-your-own sushi roll model works for this fast-paced yet casual eatery. And, if you're a sushi fan already, then you can't roll by without stopping in.

1914 University Blvd., 205-331-4542
ajiansushi.com

DELIGHT IN AUTHENTIC MEXICAN FARE
AT CENTRAL MESA

Located in the heart of Tuscaloosa's downtown, Central Mesa quietly continues to do what they do best: made-from-scratch, reimagined, classic Mexican dishes. Of course, they do margaritas pretty well too, earning a nod from AL.com for one of the state's top 12 must-try margs. Offering brunch and dinner with a lively vibe, thanks to a dining room strongly influenced by Dia de los Muertos (Day of the Dead), Central Mesa toes the line for Mexican-inspired dining experiences. In-house, freshly made tortillas make all the difference, especially when loaded with slow-roasted meats and lots of veggies. Choosing an entrée can be a chore, but you can't go wrong with specialty tacos, chimichangas, or steak burritos. Tres leches is where it's at as far as sweet meal-ending treats, so save some room for at least one to share. It's worth the calories.

519 Greensboro Ave., 205-523-7738
eatcentralmesa.com

BRING ON THE DRINKS
AT BLACK WARRIOR
BREWING COMPANY

When friendships and a passion for brewing collide, dreams become reality. Jason Spikes, Joe Fuller, and Eric Hull spent long weekends in a basement perfecting recipes and improving their beers. During that season, they met Wayne Yarbrough, who eventually rounded out their four-man team. One November day, they found an old barbershop on University Boulevard and knew it was the place where they'd put down roots for their dream. Engineering and construction day jobs gave them the skills they'd need to turn this run-down shop into a brewery, and Thanksgiving week 2012, they signed a lease for this property that would someday be Black Warrior Brewing Company. Almost 12 months later, the doors opened, and the first beers were poured. And, the rest, as they say, is history. Today, Black Warrior Brewing invites travelers, friends, and locals to stop by the brewery and taproom for a cold beer and a look around.

2216 University Blvd., 205-248-7841
blackwarriorbrewing.com

RENDEZVOUS ON A ROOFTOP BAR

Roll Call
The Alamite Hotel
2321 6th St., 205-794-8270
rollcalltcl.com

The 205 Tuscaloosa
2451 Jack Warner Pkwy., 205-498-0089
the205tuscaloosa.com

The Lookout Rooftop Bar
Hotel Indigo, 111 Greensboro Ave., 205-535-3987

BUILD A BLOODY MARY
AT BRICK & SPOON

A completely satisfying experience awaits at Brick & Spoon with a fun and funky menu featuring breakfast, brunch, and lunch dishes that are the talk of the town. Choices are as entertaining as they are appetizing with breakfast selections like Bananas in Pajamas (crispy banana egg rolls and Foster sauce), Crab Cake Benny (bacon-sautéed spinach, poached eggs, and house-made hollandaise, served with fire-roasted corn grits), Café beignets, pancakes, and a host of other all-American favorites. Lunch is a smorgasbord of burgers and fries, samiches, chicken, and seafood. Pair your fare with a lovely cocktail or take advantage of Brick & Spoon's build-your-own Bloody Mary service. Pick your vodka, veggies, spices, meat, cheese, and rimmer for a concoction made perfectly to your liking. If you fall in love with their pepper sauce or Bloody Mary mix, you can buy some to take with you. Now that's a souvenir!

2318 4th St., 205-345-5551
brickandspoon.com/location/tuscaloosa-al

EAT AUTHENTICALLY
AT ANTOJITOS IZCALLI

Don't be fooled by the exterior of Antojitos Izcalli. Open only since 2017, this little taste of Mexico tucked away in a strip mall was named the best Latin food in Alabama by Buzzfeed and Yelp in 2019. Come for mouthwatering, authentic Mexican dishes like street tacos, horchata, torta Cubana, or steak quesadilla—it's all good! There's usually a daily special as well as a good selection of kid-friendly options, and if you're the lucky sort, you might be there on an apple salad or fried Oreo day. There's not a lot of seating in this little restaurant, so it's common to have a wait. No worries, however; it is 100 percent worth it. Locals rave about the quality of food and the wonderful service, but decide for yourself. Dine in or order to go, but don't sleep on this Tuscaloosa dining gem just off of McFarland Boulevard.

623 Hargrove E Rd., 205-331-4226

FEED YOUR ADVENTURE
WITH FLAVORS OF THE BLACK BELT

Southerners are known for having an adventurous side. And, when it involves food, and a trail, it's even better. This one is almost too good to be true. Tuscaloosa proudly claims its place as part of the "Ques 'N' Brews" Black Belt trail that takes participants on a journey through the back roads of Tuscaloosa and Pickens County. You'll receive tips for finding flavorful foods, a bounty of brews, a shopping checklist, recommendations for where to stay, and lots of adventure along the way. Head over to the website below, and download the passport and resource guide. Scroll down and click on "Ques 'N' Brews" for everything you could possibly need to know for a long weekend of fun and frolic. Turn it up a notch by gathering friends and going in one big adventurous group.

alabamablackbeltadventures.org/road-trips/flavors-of-the-black-belt

TIP

Want more foodie adventures along Alabama's Black Belt? There are nine trails in all and each has a different theme. Ready-made weekend trips await!

Baker's Confections Are Sweet Perfection
Sumter, Hale, and Greene Counties

Divine Sausages Rival Devil Dogs
Butler, Conecuh, and Crenshaw Counties

Donuts Galore & French Swirls
Barbour, Bullock, and Pike Counties

Cheesy Bites . . . Smokin' Sauces
Perry, Dallas, and Lowndes Counties

Fish Kings & Pepper Jelly Queens
Choctaw and Marengo Counties

Ques 'N' Brews
Tuscaloosa and Pickens Counties

Scout for Tasty Treasures
Clarke, Monroe, and Wilcox Counties

Spirits on the Plains
Lee and Russell Counties

Syrup Makin 'N' Bacon Jammin
Montgomery and Macon Counties

alabamablackbeltadventures.org/road-trips/flavors-of-the-black-belt

Tuscaloosa Barnyard
courtesy of Visit Tuscaloosa

MUSIC
AND ENTERTAINMENT

CATCH A CONCERT
AT MERCEDES-BENZ AMPHITHEATER

The Mercedes-Benz Amphitheater, owned and operated by the City of Tuscaloosa, is West Alabama's largest outdoor theater and sits on 15 lovely acres of the Black Warrior Riverbanks. In close proximity to both restaurants and shops of downtown and UA campus, the amphitheater is poised for convenience and packages the perfect date night. Arts and entertainment are aplenty at the amphitheater, voted by *Alabama Magazine* as the No. 1 amphitheater in the state for the 2018 "Best of Bama" awards. Each year the venue hosts Celebration on the River, a free Fourth of July celebration that includes the Tuscaloosa Symphony Orchestra. Fantastic concerts are frequent throughout the year, and chances are, one of your musical favorites may be coming soon. Keep your finger on the pulse of Mercedes-Benz Amphitheater events by visiting the website below.

2710 Jack Warner Pkwy., 205-248-5280
mercedesbenzamphitheater.com

BRING ON THE COMEDY
AT ALCOVE INTERNATIONAL TAVERN

This upscale neighborhood bar and tavern opened in an off-the-beaten-path location with the purpose of giving folks a different kind of choice in local bar scenes. Popularity increased as the smallest bar in town somehow offered the largest beer selection. Interior design is not the normal neon bar signs, but rather artwork imported from Peru plus one dedicated room for local artists. Charming, yet unexpected.

Every Friday night, Alcove showcases bands from around the Southeast beginning at 10 p.m. They also host Stand Up Tuscaloosa (local comedy) the second Wednesday of the month with open mic night at 9 p.m. Lastly, come on the fourth Saturday of each month for the live comedy showcase at 9 p.m., featuring local comedians and/or a headliner who is just passing through town. There's no cover charge for these events, but like the bar, you must be 21 and older to be admitted for any of these functions.

730 22nd Ave., 205-469-9110
alcovetavern.com

TIP

If you love the bar scene, but not the smoke, remember that Alcove is a smoke-free bar establishment. Smoking is, however, permitted outside on the patios.

DRINK (CRAFT BEER) AND BE HAPPY
AT DRUID CITY BREWING COMPANY

Serving the local scene since 2012, Druid City Brewing Company is Tuscaloosa's original craft brewery. Get a glimpse of local art along with weekly events (live music, open mic night, music bingo, and trivia)—it's all on their lively and frequently updated Facebook page. Enjoy one of their own brews or something from the cider side. Bar foods range from tacos and loaded nachos to pizza, chili dogs, and other servings from the kitchen guaranteed to cause a multiple-napkin event. Not a drinker? They have zero-proof options sure to please, like kombucha and hop-infused sparkling water. Always entertaining, Druid City does a great job of pleasing their customers with a tagline of: Come see what's cookin' at Ell's Kitchen! Brews, good bar food, and entertainment . . . what more could you ask for?

700 14th St., 205-342-0051
facebook.com/druidcitybrewingcompany

OTHER T-TOWN BARS AND BREWERIES KNOWN FOR MUSIC AND ENTERTAINMENT

Atomic Cocktail Bar
Live music shows, video game nights, and trivia contests
Lower level of Dillard's Chophouse, 2330 4th St., 205-614-8782
dillardschophouse.com

Big Al's
Live music, dancing, and pool tournaments
2108 14th Ave., 205-759-9180

Copper Top
Live music and happy-hour specials
2300 4th St., 205-343-6867
facebook.com/thecoppertoptuscaloosa

Loosa Brews
412 20th Ave., 205-737-7440
loosabrews.com

Nocturnal Tavern
2209 4th St.
facebook.com/nocturnaltavern

Rhythm & Brews
2308 4th St., 205-657-8700
rhythmandbrewstuscaloosa-al.com

Rounders
1215 University Blvd., 205-345-4848
roundersonthestrip.com

The Rabbit Hole
Live music shows, cornhole, and an eclectic hangout
1407 University Blvd., 205-549-5076
facebook.com/therabbitholetusc

DANCE AND DINE IN A FORMER TRAIN STATION
AT DRUID CITY SOCIAL

Druid City Social brings a story of evolution, history, and preservation, as the building was once an L&N train station, a private event center, and multiple eateries. When the pandemic happened, it was operating as 301 Bistro, and just as other restaurants, they had to make changes to keep the doors open. Current owner Bill Lloyd teamed up with Brandon Hanks of Downtown Entertainment to create Druid City Social, a new concept that seemed to hit the sweet spot for what Tuscaloosa was lacking in the entertainment realm. Large outdoor spaces became gathering places as large-screen TVs and a stage were added to the biergarten, making it perfect for live music and concerts. The inside got a sound and screen upgrade to create the best in game-day experiences. Best of all, customers can still get good food (burgers, sandwiches, salads, and more sophisticated dishes) alongside craft cocktails and other libations.

301 Greensboro Ave., 205-248-2704
druidcitysocial.com

TIP

Keep up with upcoming events at Druid City Social on Instagram (@dc_social_). Most tickets may be purchased through Eventbrite in advance or at the door.

TAP YOUR TOES
TO LIVE TUNES
AT DRUID CITY MUSIC HALL

It all started in 1940 when a bowling alley sat on the 1307 University Boulevard property anchoring the downtown area. Almost 30 years later, the demand was more for film, and a two-screen theater emerged. Eventually, the venue began hosting live music events under several different names, and in 2020 following an extensive renovation and construction project, Druid City Music Hall found its groove. With a functional backstage area that included several dressing rooms and a large green room—as well as upgrades to the stage, bars, and bathrooms—the music venue was able to attract many popular musicians and bands. And they've kept on coming. Performers like Zac Brown Band, Jason Isbell, Luke Bryan, Luke Combs, and Dave Matthews have graced this stage. You can keep tabs on what events are next by clicking the SHOWS button on their website.

1307 University Blvd., 205-462-3323
druidcitymusichall.com

UNLEASH THE ARTIST IN YOUR CHILD
AT THE ART GARAGE

Visiting the Tuscaloosa area isn't all about sporting events or things only adults will love. Bring the family along and check out cool spots like the Art Garage, an art studio for children! Owner Joanna Lemmon taught children for years, and when her family relocated to Tuscaloosa, she immediately discovered what the college town needed. She got right to work scoping out a place where children and babies (even adults!) could explore art in an exciting yet uninhibited way. Hence, Art Garage was born. Opportunities include hour-long open play sessions, weekly classes, events, and birthday parties. For open play, you need to make a reservation so that art helpers and supplies will be available for your child. Note that open play is only available during studio hours. What a great way to bring out the artistic nature in your little one!

2422 6th St., 205-523-5506
artgaragetuscaloosa.com

GATHER
THE CREW FOR FUN
AT GOVERNMENT PLAZA

Government Plaza is a five-acre park in the heart of Tuscaloosa's downtown district where, depending on the season, folks gather for entertainment and activities. Summertime brings Live at the Plaza, a popular Friday night live music series plus a Kid Zone loaded with fun stuff for the younger ones. Bring a blanket and chairs if you like. It's pet friendly, too! November ushers in a different kind of fun with the spectacular Holidays on the Plaza event, complete with ice-skating, a tinsel trail, and other holiday festivities.

Stay abreast of the plaza events schedule as there are other available opportunities for family entertainment throughout the year. Summer movies are always a hit. And, the Druid City Arts Festival, usually in the springtime, features artists from across the Southeast, live music, kid-friendly activities, food trucks, and a beer garden. There's never a dull moment at the plaza!

6th St., 205-248-5311
tuscaloosa.com/latp
holidaysontheplaza.com

HOLD A BABY CHICK
AT TUSCALOOSA BARNYARD

If you've ever struggled finding things to do with your children while traveling, this one is for you! Tuscaloosa Barnyard offers so much family-friendly fun with a petting zoo, horse and tractor rides, cornhole, and so many more hands-on activities. Spend the day letting the kids rule the roost while learning to milk a cow, holding baby chicks, playing in the corn crib, riding pedal karts, and in warm months, swimming and enjoying a splash pad. In the fall they have pumpkins for sale, and December brings Christmas on the Farm. The barnyard also has a summer camp, swim lessons, birthday parties, and field trips. Buy your tickets online and save a little time. General admission covers feeding the fish and ducks, as well as feeding grains to the farm animals.

11453 Turner Bridge Rd., 205-454-8841
tuscaloosabarnyard.com

CATCH A PERFORMANCE
AT BAMA THEATRE

An integral part of the local arts scene, the Bama Theatre is located alongside restaurants and other entertainment venues in the downtown district of Tuscaloosa. The historic theater, established through Public Works Administration funding in 1938, is currently managed by the Arts Council and showcases the Bama Art House Film Series, Acoustic Nights, and various other concerts and performances. Designer/architect David O. Whilldin chose elements associated with Roman architecture for the Bama Theatre building, but contrasted with an interior he referred to as a Mediterranean Palazzo during the Italian Renaissance. Listed on the National Register of Historic Places, the Bama Theatre offers an amazing ambiance for theatrical and dance performances, concerts, recitals, and art exhibitions. Check the website often for a complete listing of coming events along with a link to purchase tickets.

600 Greensboro Ave., 205-758-5195
tuscarts.org/bama

TIP

If you love community theater, check out
Theatre Tuscaloosa for opportunities to see
fantastic performances with one of the largest
community theaters in the state.

9500 Old Greensboro Rd., 205-391-2277
theatretusc.com

UNWIND
AT THE VENUE TUSCALOOSA

What a fabulous notion to have multiple restaurants (including a bar and Sweet Shoppe) plus live music and other family-friendly entertainment all in one venue! For founders Bryan and Lee Finison, it just makes sense as they are raising a large family themselves, so they get it. The Venue Tuscaloosa offers five restaurants surrounding the lawn and patio with plenty of seating, games, and space to relax watching main-stage entertainment. It's a good bet that you'll find food to suit every palate (even the pickiest child), and finish off your meal with ice cream and milkshakes. If you are visiting Tuscaloosa for a travel ball tournament, Kentuck, or another activity, this is the perfect eat-and-hang-out place between events. Feel free to move tables together to make room for the whole gang—group size is no problem here. Bring the family and stay as long as you like!

6052 Watermelon Rd., Northport, 205-523-4440
venuetuscaloosa.com

CELEBRATE GERMAN HERITAGE
AT OKTOBERFEST & 5K

Tuscaloosa loves a reason to celebrate, and October begs for a beer festival, so Oktoberfest makes perfect sense! Many local residents were born and raised in Germany, and it has become a popular tradition to host this annual festival to draw folks together for a day of family-friendly activities, contests, music, food, and beer in downtown Tuscaloosa. In conjunction with Oktoberfest, there is a 5K race for charity. Stops at replenishing stations along the way will prove to be slightly out of character from "normal" refueling stations. Be prepared to nibble on pretzels and sausage while you rehydrate. Runners receive free entry into Oktoberfest as well as their first beer for free (provided they are 21-plus years old). Oktoberfest is held annually at Druid City Social. Each year, the date and other pertinent information is posted on the website, so check often and don't miss this fun experience.

tuscaloosaoktoberfest.com

ROSIN UP YOUR BOW AND GET READY
FOR THE FIDDLE FEST EVENT

Each February, the Fiddle Fest event comes to the Martin Campus of Shelton State Community College. Bluegrass sounds fill the air as musicians battle for a chunk of the prize money, which is split up into several categories ranging from fiddles, guitars, and mandolins to buck dancing, banjo, and bands. It's a family-friendly event with arts, crafts, food vendors, and other family activities. Sponsors from across West Alabama fund this event through sponsorships in hopes of preserving this piece of musical history. If you are interested in attending this fun festival, keep a check on the website for dates, times, vendors, and contestants. And, if you have some talent in this realm, maybe you'd like to register to *be* a contestant. Come on now! Rosin up that bow and let's get this party started!

Martin Campus of Shelton State Community College
9500 Old Greensboro Rd., 205-391-2211
thefiddlefest.com

CHALLENGE YOURSELF
AT ESCAPE TUSCALOOSA

Following a huge trend in the entertainment industry, escape rooms seem to be popping up in every town across the country. And why not? It's great, affordable entertainment for a birthday celebration, ladies' night out, team building, date night, or just a fun escape (no pun intended). Escape Tuscaloosa is a five-star boutique escape game experience with three authentic rooms creating challenging situations for adventure seekers. With a slightly different twist, Escape Tuscaloosa offers varying levels of play as well as multiroom experiences. Stay up to date with current room and theme opportunities, as well as pricing and times available, by checking the website for dates when you will be visiting the Tuscaloosa area. Get ready to pool your knowledge, wit, and skill for a successful outing at Escape!

The Galleria of Tuscaloosa
1663 McFarland N Blvd., Ste. G2, 205-248-2115
escapetuscaloosa.com

Lake Lurleen
courtesy of Visit Tuscaloosa

SPORTS
AND RECREATION

GET FIRED UP FOR FOOTBALL
AT BRYANT-DENNY STADIUM

If you're in town for a game-day experience, planning is crucial. Choosing restaurants, events, activities, and apparel that resonate with Crimson Tide football will build your momentum for the big game. Start your adventure with breakfast at the Waysider to fuel up for the day. Consider shopping on the strip to find game-day attire, then grab a pregame Yellow Hammer drink at Gallettes. Spend some time at the Paul W. Bryant Museum to soak up some University of Alabama football history and prepare your mind for victory. Plan to tailgate on the Quad or walk over to the north end of the stadium for Champion's Lane with music, autograph signings, and food trucks. Catch the Walk of Champions and the Elephant Stomp featuring the Million Dollar Band, and you're ready to head to your seat inside legendary Bryant-Denny Stadium. Practice your battle cry . . . ROLL TIDE ROLL . . . and bring home a win!

920 Paul W. Bryant Dr., 205-348-3600
rolltide.com/sports/2016/6/10/facilities-bryant-denny-html.aspx

TIP

For information on free Quad tailgating on the west side, visit uagameday.com and click tailgating. Still need tickets? Check out rolltide.com or seatgeek.com/alabama-crimson-tide-football-tickets.

FOLLOW YOUR FAVORITE SPORT
AT THE UNIVERSITY OF ALABAMA

While the University of Alabama has quite a collection of National Championships with Crimson Tide football, there are plenty of other award-winning sports teams that are legends in their own right. Each has amassed its own fan base and traditions while continuing to carry the same spirit of competition and excellence that the University of Alabama is famous for. Don your crimson and white, choose a sporting event, and help the Tide roll to victory!

Baseball
Men's and women's basketball
Football
Men's and women's golf
Gymnastics
Rowing
Women's soccer
Softball
Swimming and diving
Men's and women's tennis
Men's and women's Track and field/cross country
Volleyball

Find out more about these sports including rosters
and schedules at rolltide.com.

GET BACK TO NATURE
AT LAKE LURLEEN STATE PARK

For years, locals and visitors alike have packed a picnic basket and headed to Lake Lurleen State Park for outdoor adventures galore. Just northwest of Tuscaloosa, this 1,625-acre park surrounds beautiful Lake Lurleen and shares many amenities with park visitors. If the charm of sleeping outside sounds exciting, the campground may be just your spot offering 91 modern campsites with both water and electric hookup. There are pavilions, a beach and bathhouse, fishing piers, boat rentals, hiking and biking trails, a nature center, paddleboats, and much more. If fishing is your jam, it's important to note that the 250-acre lake is stocked with largemouth bass, bream, catfish, and crappie. Some 23 miles of trails run alongside the shores of Lake Lurleen where mountain bikers are as welcome as hikers. Perfect for everyone in the family, days (and nights) are well spent at Lake Lurleen State Park.

13226 Lake Lurleen Rd., Coker, 205-339-1558
alapark.com/parks/lake-lurleen-state-park

TIP
There is a helpful park brochure on the website available for viewing or downloading. Consider using this resource.
alapark.com/parks/lake-lurleen-state-park

HIT THE LINKS
AT OL' COLONY GOLF COMPLEX

Bring your sticks and hit the links at award-winning Ol' Colony Golf Course, a par-72 championship public course with up to 6,494 yards of golf and a driving range to hone your skills. Designed by Jerry Pate, the 18-hole course showcases well-kept Bermuda grass fairways and greens, along with 25 acres of lakes that sometimes present a challenge to golfers. Find golf clothing, equipment, and accessories readily available in the pro shop and concessions at the Bounce Back Grille. The Brion Hardin Teaching Facility offers a state-of-the-art Trackman Launch Monitor, V1 Pro Software, and Explaner Plane System (swing training). Meet John Gray, director of golf and winner of the 2019 Bill Strausbaugh Award presented by the Alabama/Northwest Florida Section Professional Golfers' Association (PGA). Golf enthusiasts will thoroughly enjoy playing 18 holes on the official home course of the University of Alabama golf team. Can I get a "Roll Tide"?

401 Old Colony Rd., 205-562-3201
golf.tcpara.org

WORK ON YOUR GOLF GAME
AT THESE ADDITIONAL LOCAL COURSES

Hidden Meadows Golf Course
Public course with 18 holes.
13000 Old Cove Rd., Northport, 205-339-3673
golflink.com/golf-courses/al/northport/hidden-meadows-golf-course

Tall Pines Golf Club
Semiprivate course with 18 holes and a driving range.
5604 Woodland Forrest Dr., 205-556-1232
tallpinesgolfclubal.com

Bonus: **Bowers Park** offers a disc golf course, and while very different from golf with clubs, it is a trendy sport that offers a lot of fun with a competitive spirit. Consider it!
1600 James I. Harrision Jr. Pkwy. E, 205-562-3200
tcpara.org/p/bowers-park

WATCH WATER-SKI COMPETITIONS
AT LYMANLAND

Once upon a time Lyman Hardy, a water-skiing aficionado, yearned for a place in the Tuscaloosa area where skiers could enjoy water recreation without bumping into fishermen or Jet Skis. In 1992, he decided to build his own private lake. Tucked into the small community of Duncanville, just outside of Tuscaloosa, Hardy's man-made lake was designed particularly for skiing at almost half a mile in length, eight feet in depth, and narrow like a football field. In 2000, Lymanland became the practice facility for the University of Alabama's Water-Ski Club in addition to their home for tournaments. And, in 2008 Lymanland hosted its first water-ski tournament with help from Tuscaloosa Travel and Tourism. Today, Lymanland attracts professional skiers from all over the country for competition skiing, and the public is welcome to come and watch. Check the website for events, times, and admission prices.

15865 Waterski Ln., Duncanville
visittuscaloosa.com/one-and-only-lymanland-water-skiing-heaven

TRAVEL RESOURCES TO HELP PLAN YOUR LEGENDARY TRIP

Tuscaloosa Visitor's Guide
A free trip-planning resource in digital or hard-copy format.
205-391-9200
visittuscaloosa.com/#visitors-guide

Tuscaloosa Newsletter
Stay in the know with Tuscaloosa happenings.
205-391-9200
visittuscaloosa.com

Alabama Tourism Department
A wealth of information is available by searching
Tuscaloosa on their site.
334-242-4169
alabama.travel

STRIKE UP A GOOD TIME
AT BOWLERO TUSCALOOSA

Gather your friends and head to Bowlero for a fun-filled evening at the company's first Alabama location. Novice or pro, you'll notice the striking (no pun intended) appearance that sets this bowling alley apart from others with great use of lighting, seating, decor, and offerings beyond the lanes. The Bowlero experience includes blackl-ight bowling and a state-of-the-art arcade, plus food and drink options you won't be expecting. Sip on mixologist-inspired cocktails while noshing on wings, party nachos, mozzarella sticks, and such.

In close proximity to University Mall, Bowlero is convenient and lively. Reserve a lane and find discounts on their website. Also, keep in mind, Bowlero Tuscaloosa is an 18-plus facility every day after 7 p.m. unless accompanied by a parent or legal guardian.

2001 McFarland Blvd. E, 205-518-7781
bowlero.com/location/bowlero-tuscaloosa

STAY FIT
AT FAUCETT BROTHERS ACTIVITY CENTER, ROCK WALL, AND POOL

Work in time for fitness and exercise even when traveling with a stop at Faucett Brothers Activity Center, Rock Wall, and Pool. At Tuscaloosa's go-to for family fun, regulars and visitors enjoy lots of activity choices including state-of-the-art fitness equipment (must be 13-plus years old), a game room, indoor swimming pool (therapeutic and lap), indoor walking track, outdoor climbing boulder, indoor rock wall, and more. Take a class, play pickleball, or play volleyball. The activity center offers day passes and childcare for those who need it. Stop by King's Kitchen on Hargrove Road for the best in comfort foods like burgers, sandwiches, and fried chicken with great sides. Grab your favorites and plan to have lunch at one of the activity center's picnic tables. Who doesn't love a picnic, right?

13040 Eugenia Faucett Dr., Northport, 205-331-5600
tcpara.org/p/faucett-brothers-activity-center

PICNIC AND PLAY
AT A LOCAL PARK

Perfect picnic spots and playgrounds for children are in no short supply as Tuscaloosa offers a myriad of park experiences. Here are a few.

Annette M. Shelby Park Path: Enjoy a paved path for walking or biking plus a playground, splash pad, and restrooms. Bring a blanket for picnicking.

Harrison Taylor Splash Pad in Palmore Park: Open from Memorial Day to Labor Day, you'll find a splash pad, restrooms, and water available.

Lake Lurleen State Park: This state park offers designated picnic areas and pavilions, as well as fishing, camping, hiking, and boating.

Monnish Park: Here your family will enjoy picnic tables, electricity, restrooms, a grill and playground.

The Randall Family Park and Trailhead: You'll find this park located at the Northern Riverwalk with a trailhead, recreational path, playground, and pavilion.

Van De Graaff Arboretum & Historic Bridge Park: Among the facility's amenities there are picnic tables, a grill, trails, overnight camping, fishing, boating, hiking, restrooms, and the famous King Bowstring Bridge.

Annette M. Shelby Park Path
1614 15th St.
alltrails.com/trail/us/alabama/annette-m-shelby-park-path

Harrison Taylor Splash Pad in Palmore Park
3701 Fosters Ferry Rd., 659-256-1002
tcpara.org/p/harrison-taylor-splash-pad

Lake Lurleen State Park
13226 Lake Lurleen Rd., Coker, 205-339-1558
alapark.com/lake-lurleen-state-park

Monnish Park
1500 Hackberry Ln., 205-562-3210
tcpara.org/p/monnish-park

The Randall Family Park and Trailhead
201 Rice Mine Rd. Loop, 205-248-5311
visittuscaloosa.com/listing/randall-family-park-and-trailhead

Van De Graaff Arboretum & Historic Bridge Park
3231 Robert Cardinal Airport Rd., Northport, 205-799-4038
tcpara.org/p/van-de-graaff-arboretum

TEST YOUR SKILLS
AT CRUX CLIMBING

A local bouldering gym, Crux Climbing is *the* place for climbing aficionados. Having this specific place to foster community with like-minded people is especially important for locally owned Crux, where promoting a space for climbers to reach new goals is paramount. Visit on a day pass and invest in honing your skills using varying types of climbing walls at this indoor training facility of sorts. New to the sport? You'll find lots of support at Crux and perhaps return for a competitive event one day. With few options in the Tuscaloosa area to explore this activity, Crux has proven to be a crowd-pleaser, not only for enthusiasts but also for team building and parties. Trendy and a great form of exercise. Try your hand at climbing!

1790 Harper Rd., Northport, 205-561-6133
cruxclimbingal.com

LACE UP YOUR SNEAKERS TO WALK, BIKE, AND PLAY
ON THE RIVERWALK

Beginning at Capitol Park and ending at a Manderson Landing gazebo, you'll find a nice, paved, four-and-a-half-mile trail just perfect for outdoor recreation. Lots of parks are scattered across the trail and most are dog friendly, a plus if you are traveling with a furry companion. There's a playground near the library along with a splash pad for the kiddos at the Bama Bell dock, and an abundance of resting places (benches, gazebos, and trees that beg for hammocks) throughout the trail. Bring a picnic, a bike, or both! The Riverwalk is a wonderful place to spend some time, plus streetlamps keep the night trail bright. The path itself is clearly divided by a painted line creating a two-way road for bikers and walkers. It is best to take advantage of parking at the amphitheater and start your loop there, so keep that in mind. Don't forget your sneakers!

2710 Jack Warner Pkwy., 205-562-3220
visittuscaloosa.com/listing/the-riverwalk

STOP AND SMELL THE FLOWERS
AT THE UNIVERSITY OF ALABAMA
ARBORETUM

As an affiliate of the University of Alabama Museums, UA Arboretum is an important asset to the Department of Biological Sciences in the College of Arts and Sciences. Maintaining plant specimens and collections, the arboretum is charged with furthering botanical education to those who visit as well as students on campus. Making its home on land donated by the federal government, the arboretum has much to offer with walking trails that navigate a native woodland section, various gardens, and a collection of ornamental plants. A Nick's Kids donation made it possible for the Arboretum to upgrade the children's garden to include accessible picnic tables and play elements. This much-needed enhancement will afford more families a chance to utilize the garden, and increase local preschool outreach programs. When in town, go by and see what's growing on at the UA Arboretum!

4801 Arboretum Way, 205-553-3278
arboretum.ua.edu

GEAR UP FOR FUN ON THE WATER
WITH TUSCALOOSA PADDLEBOARD RENTALS

Join the latest trend for adventure on the water with paddleboards. Affordable and high-quality boards are available from Tuscaloosa Paddleboard Rentals and, for convenience, they may be picked up or delivered for a small fee. Non-strenuous but a decent workout, paddleboarding is perfect fun in the summertime for all ages. Tuscaloosa Paddleboard Rentals offers individual and group rates in addition to hourly and party rates. Reserve your board in advance to ensure availability and get ready to paddle your cares away on the waters of Tuscaloosa. Current areas served are the dock at Riverwalk Condominiums, Lake Nicol Park, and other local areas upon request. For up-to-date information such as weather and pickup locations, follow along on Facebook. Isn't it time you tried a new-to-you water sport? This is your sign!

205-394-4921
tuscaloosapaddleboard.com

CAST A LINE
AT LAKE TUSCALOOSA

If water recreation is your thing, Lake Tuscaloosa is the place for you! Constructed as an additional water supply for local residents and for industrial use, the popular lake is easily accessible and enjoyed for boating, swimming, and fishing by many. Just north of both Tuscaloosa and Northport, the 5,885-acre water supply reservoir boasts 177 miles of shoreline. If you're looking to throw a line, the tailwater area (North River) that runs into the Black Warrior River basin is a common place to go, as well as Binion and Turkey Creeks. Wondering what your catch might be? Common fish (sport and nongame) present in Lake Tuscaloosa are the Alabama spotted bass, largemouth bass, bluegill, redear sunfish, white crappie, catfish, and more. There are plenty of boat ramps and launches available to the public, and if you are planning a visit, look for Lake Tuscaloosa maps at local marinas and sporting goods stores.

650 Lake Nicol Rd., 205-349-0279
tuscaloosa.com/city-services/water/lakes

ADDITIONAL PLACES FOR WATER RECREATION

Harris Lake
This 220-acre lake offers fishing, canoeing, kayaking, paddleboarding, bird-watching, high cliffs, two dams, hiking trails, a beach, and a hidden swimming hole at the bottom of the stream coming from the waterfall of the dam.
Lake Harris Rd.
tuscaloosa.com/city-services/water/lakes

Hurricane Creek
Water and trails with picnic tables and restrooms.
7005 Old Birmingham Hwy., 205-562-3210
tcpara.org/p/hurricane-creek-park

Lake Nicol
Beautiful views, hiking trails, and perfect spots for swimming are available at Lake Nicol, along with canoeing, kayaking, paddleboarding, and fishing.
4409 Nicol Park Rd.
tuscaloosa.com/city-services/water/lakes

RUN FOR EDUCATION
AT THE TUSCALOOSA MAYOR'S CUP 5K FOR PRE-K

Since 2007, springtime in Tuscaloosa brings more than the A-Day Game. It brings an opportunity to be part of something rewarding and inspiring for pre-K children in the community. The Tuscaloosa Mayor's Cup 5K for Pre-K, presented by Mercedes-Benz US International, is indeed much more than a race. The event has raised over $300,000 for preschool resources in the Tuscaloosa area, creating more prepared kindergarteners who achieve success throughout their school years. Walkers and runners are welcome to take part in the 3.1-mile race that begins and ends in Government Plaza and is supported by a host of solid sponsors like-minded in this pre-K initiative. Register online in advance and pack your running/walking shoes. Join others in this effort that currently supports more than 650 local academically at-risk preschoolers.

Government Plaza
Downtown Tuscaloosa, 205-248-5311
tuscaloosamayorscup.com

PRACTICE YOUR BACKHAND
AT TUSCALOOSA TENNIS CENTER

If tennis is your jam, then bring those racquets along on your travels and play a set or a match at Tuscaloosa Tennis Center (TTC). A premier facility in West Alabama, TTC features all-season tennis with four outdoor hard courts, six outdoor clay courts, and three indoor courts. This award-winning facility is both membership based and open to the public. It is a good idea to reserve a court online 24 hours in advance just to be certain there is one available in your time frame. TTC offers something for every age including junior and adult lessons, clinics, mixers, leagues, and tournaments. Stop by and check out one of the state's top tennis facilities, learn how to play, or hit a few balls. It's always great to get some exercise while traveling.

715 21st Ave. E, 205-331-0211
tcpara.org/tennis

FUN FACT
Tuscaloosa Tennis Center was named "Indoor Tennis Facility of the Year" in 2015 by *Tennis Industry* magazine.

TAKE A WALKING TOUR
OF THE UNIVERSITY OF ALABAMA

Many visitors to Tuscaloosa are interested in touring the University of Alabama campus but aren't sure where to start. Here are some tips to make the most out of your visit with a self-guided tour. Starting on University Boulevard at the Quad, you'll see Denny Chimes and work your way over to Bryant-Denny Stadium, passing lots of landmarks and places to pause for pictures. A sidewalk tour will take you down sorority row in one direction and to the downtown area in the other. You can find shopping, restaurants, and entertainment downtown. Remember that while the campus is along University Boulevard, it expands farther out as well. Between Paul Bryant Drive and Jack Warner Parkway (at the river), you'll see museums like the Alabama Natural History Museum and the Paul W. Bryant Museum.

University of Alabama
University Blvd.

TIP
For help navigating streets and buildings on campus, print or download the map located at campus-maps.com/university-of-alabama.

EXPLORE DOWNTOWN
ON FOOT

Learning the lay of the land is easy when it's a walkable area like downtown Tuscaloosa. University Boulevard is the main road and offers a very comfortable stroll with lots of storefronts, bars, dining establishments, and other attractions to duck in and out of. Street signs are easy to read and well laid out. You'll see markers along the sidewalks noting places that are part of the Civil Rights Trail along with other historically significant buildings. Capitol Park is downtown close to the amphitheater and is lovely. Heading south on Greensboro Avenue will lead to the Bama Theatre, more shopping, and dining. Government Plaza is on 6th Street to the south, hosts a variety of events, and often features live music. There are benches along the walk for resting and ample parking on nongame days.

University Blvd.

STROLL THROUGH THE CHARMING HISTORIC DISTRICT
OF DRUID CITY

If you love architectural gems, historic homes, and charming neighborhoods, then head to Queen City Avenue for the loveliest district in town. Walking or driving through Druid City, notice the houses are reminiscent of yesteryear, with some dating back to the 19th century. There are bungalow-style homes, plantation homes, large front porches, small front porches, and noticeably, everything in between. It's easy to imagine them in their glory days on either side of oak tree–lined streets, wondering where the best parties would have been thrown. Continuing your walk heading north, if you go past University Boulevard, there are more wonderful old homes as you approach Queen City Park. The Warner Transportation Museum is close by as well as the Tuscaloosa Library and the River Walk. Take your time wandering through Druid City. It's fabulous and well worth the time.

Queen City Ave.
visittuscaloosa.com/listing/walk-druid-city

TIP

If you love antebellum homes like those scattered within Druid City, there are some available on Airbnb to rent while in town visiting. Search online at Airbnb.com for Tuscaloosa Antebellum homes.

GET DOWN AND DIRTY
AT TUSCALOOSA MUD PARK

The new Tuscaloosa Mud Park, 10 minutes from downtown near Hillcrest High School, is an attraction in a category all by itself. Open only on weekends, the mud park attracts visitors in search of an off-roading experience in their own vehicle, side-by-side, four-wheeler, or dirt bike. Participants come to the 10-acre park to get down and dirty on 10 different tracks, each one 400 feet or longer. Prepare for mud pits, rough terrain, and car crushing opportunities plus a freestyle water pit and 100-foot slip-n-slide. Traditional trails are ditched at Tuscaloosa Mud Park in favor of safer, centralized tracks, but have no fear, none of the thrill-seeking details have changed. There's still plenty of fun to be had at this unique venue where safety is a cornerstone. Please note that both Saturday and Sunday include some family ride time (no alcohol) and adult ride time (alcohol permitted).

8132 Old Marion Rd., 205-246-0194
visittuscaloosa.com/listing/tuscaloosa-mud-park

ENJOY AN ALL-INCLUSIVE PLAYGROUND
AT MASON'S PLACE

An all-inclusive playground is located within Sokol Park and folks love it! Mason's Place was intentionally designed so that children of all ages and abilities could play together. It's even more fun with themed, historic, and iconic Tuscaloosa landmarks included in the design. The PARA Foundation, with help from several other organizations like Nick's Kids Foundation, the City of Tuscaloosa, the City of Northport, the Tuscaloosa County Commission, the Tuscaloosa County Park & Recreation Authority, as well as individuals, families, and businesses, raised the needed cash for this project. Those funds were used to create this much-needed venue for families requiring adaptive resources for outdoor play. It's exciting that this park brings joy to so many boys and girls each day. Mason's Place is named after Barry Mason, the PARA Foundation's fundraising chair, and former board chairman.

Located within Sokol Park South
5901 Watermelon Rd., Northport, 205-562-3210
tcpara.org/p/masons-place

The Mildred Warner House

CULTURE
AND HISTORY

LEARN FROM THE PAST
AT ALABAMA MUSEUM
OF NATURAL HISTORY

One of Alabama's most treasured museums resides in Tuscaloosa on the campus of the University of Alabama in Smith Hall (named after Dr. Eugene Allen Smith, state geologist beginning in 1873). Founded in 1831, the Alabama Museum of Natural History is the state's oldest museum and houses a celebrated collection of specimens from Dr. Smith's almost 40 years of scientific research. Impressive is an understatement when it comes to the collections, exhibits, and presentations. Check out the state fossil in addition to the skull of an American mastodon dredged from the Tombigbee River. The building itself is Classical Revival style with an engaged colonnade of eight Ionic columns just over the ground floor with a full basement below. Inside, the Atrium Gallery features a stunning, sweeping staircase that leads to the Grand Gallery Exhibition Hall with Corinthian columns and a glass roof above. It's stunning and educational—a powerful combo.

427 6th Ave., 205-348-7550
almnh.museums.ua.edu

EXPLORE, CREATE, AND DISCOVER
AT CHILDREN'S HANDS-ON MUSEUM

Children's Hands-On Museum (CHOM) is filled with spaces dedicated to learning through play. Creative places where children can be themselves. Exhibits are plentiful with family experiences for newborns through 13 years old. Check the website for current exhibits, Saturday theme days, celebrations, special programs, even field trips and birthday parties! A few examples of fun and educational exhibits are below, and remember, children under 18 must be accompanied by an adult to visit CHOM.

Lil' Sprouts Farmer's Market—Gas up the farm truck and take your veggies to market.

DCH Health System—Be a doctor, nurse, or patient and learn about your body. Make an ID bracelet, see X-rays, and care for babies in the nursery.

Grandma's Attic—Dress up and pretend with things from the attic.

Space Station CHOM—Launch your imagination at Mission Space, have a lesson in NASA history, and build "sandcastles" from Mars. (Recommended for ages 7-plus)

2213 University Blvd., 205-349-4235
chomonline.org

FEEL LIKE A CHAMPION
AT PAUL W. BRYANT MUSEUM

You don't have to be a Crimson Tide fan to appreciate the Paul W. Bryant Museum. Opened in 1988, the museum is a celebration of sports history at the University of Alabama: a space created for alumni, fans, and visitors to appreciate past events that have shaped the present. Dedicated to fostering a sense of excellence and tradition, the Bryant Museum displays artifacts following the evolution of University of Alabama football. A replica of Coach Bryant's office is a well-loved exhibit that past- and present-day fans will find tugging on their Roll Tide heartstrings.

Museum archives have served as a valuable resource for building state-of-the-art displays with videos that give a good look at players and games throughout the years. Statues, jerseys, trophies, and the like round out the cause for smiles while visiting the museum. A little education mixed with a hefty dose of memorabilia is just the recipe for a successful tourism icon.

300 Paul W. Bryant Dr., 866-772-2327
bryantmuseum.com

TIP

Save money and experience five of Tuscaloosa's best museums/attractions with one ticket via Alabama's All-in-One Ticket program. It includes admission to Alabama Museum of Natural History, Gorgas House Museum, Paul W. Bryant Museum, Moundville Archaeological Park, and Lake Lurleen State Park.

visittuscaloosa.com/all-in-one-ticket

EXPERIENCE THE ART VIBE
AT UNIVERSITY OF ALABAMA
CAMPUS GALLERIES

There are so many fabulous art galleries in the Tuscaloosa area and a few of them are actually located on the campus of the University of Alabama. Visit them in person or virtually and see the wonders of art in gallery form, as well as the many collections and changing exhibits. (Note: these are not the only UA art galleries in town, just the ones located on campus.)

Sarah Moody Gallery of Art
103 Garland Hall, 700 Capstone Dr., 205-348-1891
art.ua.edu/category/smga

Sella-Granata Art Gallery
109 Woods Hall, 7th Ave., 205-348-1893
art.ua.edu/venue/sella-granata-art-gallery

UA Public Sculpture
The University of Alabama has quite the collection of outdoor, public sculpture.
Department of Art and Art History at the University of Alabama
307 Garland Hall, 205-348-5967
art.ua.edu/galleries/ua-public-sculpture

Visiting Artists and Scholars Listing
A listing of visiting artists and lecturers including curators, critics, and scholars is available to the public.
art.ua.edu/resources/visiting-artists

VISIT THE ART GALLERIES
AT DINAH WASHINGTON
CULTURAL ARTS CENTER

Housed in the former Allen & Jemison Co. Hardware building, the Dinah Washington Cultural Arts Center is a shining example of a city cornerstone that maintains spaces for community gatherings among artists, educators, and others for work, rehearsals, creative thinking, and art purposes. With plenty of room, the DWCAC houses a multitude of office space, the Alabama Power Grand Hall, the Rotary Club of Tuscaloosa Black Box Theatre, the Arts Council Gallery, and the University of Alabama Gallery (the latter with rotating exhibits). The DWCAC is managed by the Arts Council and considered to be paramount for the arts and culture movement in downtown Tuscaloosa. Check the online schedule of events and drop by for an art viewing. You can also find them participating in the First Friday Art Walk each month.

620 Greensboro Ave., 205-345-9801
cac.tuscarts.org/contactus.php

FUN FACT

Cultural Arts Center namesake Dinah Washington, a jazz and blues vocalist and pianist, was born in Tuscaloosa. She is often referred to as the "Queen of Blues," and the most popular black female recording artist of the 1950s. She was inducted to both the Alabama Jazz Hall of Fame and the Rock and Roll Hall of Fame.

HEAR THE BELLS
AT DENNY CHIMES

Chances are, if you are around the University of Alabama campus, you'll hear Denny Chimes long before you see it. Through student fundraising efforts, Denny Chimes was erected in 1929 in honor of Dr. George Denny, university president from 1912 to 1936 and 1941 to 1942. Standing tall at 115 feet, Denny Chimes can be found on the south side of the Quad at UA. The freestanding bell tower houses a carillon of 25 brass bells that sound upon the hour and play concerts, patriotic songs, memorial tributes, and, of course, the school fight song and alma mater. The beloved UA icon was dedicated on May 27, 1929, and has since been enjoyed by students, locals, and visitors to Tuscaloosa. Walks across the Quad are all the more special when the chimes sound.

739 University Blvd., 205-348-6010
ua.edu/about/traditions

FUN FACT

Most credit Dr. George Denny, with his prudent financial management, as having one of the most significant periods of growth in university history. His tenure saw advancement campus-wide adding major buildings, fraternity and sorority houses, and student growth from 400 to almost 5,000, as well as expansion within the football program.

Yea Alabama!

Yea, Alabama! Drown 'em Tide!
Every 'Bama man's behind you,
Hit your stride.
Go teach the Bulldogs to behave,
Send the Yellow Jackets to a watery grave.
And if a man starts to weaken,
That's a shame!
For Bama's pluck and grit have
Writ her name in Crimson flame.
Fight on, fight on, fight on men!
Remember the Rose Bowl, we'll win then.
So roll on to victory,
Hit your stride,
You're Dixie's football pride,
Crimson Tide, Roll Tide, Roll Tide!

EXPERIENCE LOCAL ARTISTS AND GALLERIES
AT FIRST FRIDAY ART WALK

Enjoy food, drinks, and fabulous art at Tuscaloosa First Friday Art Walk featuring local artists, downtown galleries, and live music. Participants may vary, but a general list is below. Be sure and check each website to see hours of operation for Art Walk, exhibit information, and offerings.

firstfridaytuscaloosa.com

Dinah Washington Cultural Arts Center
Exhibit openings at both the Arts Council and the University of Alabama Galleries in the Dinah Washington Cultural Arts Center take place on First Fridays from 5 to 8 p.m. and are free.
620 Greensboro Ave., 205-345-9801
cac.tuscarts.org

Druid City Makerspace
They will have the laser cutter/engraver running and you can take home a wooden Alabama magnet.
409 23rd Ave., 205-304-1785
druidcitymakerspace.com

Harrison Galleries LLC
Deals in 19th- and 20th-century paintings, prints, drawings, and sculpture as well as vintage and contemporary photography.
Receptions take place on First Friday from 6 to 9 p.m.
2315 University Blvd., 205-464-0054
Facebook: Harrison-Galleries

Lorrie Lane Studio
A fine-art gallery and studio, representing the work of Lorrie Lane, Liz Lane, Steve Davis, and other Southeastern artists. Lorrie's painting studio is open to see art in progress.
2420 6th St., 205-292-3177
lorrielaneart.com

The Art Garage
The Art Garage is an art studio for kids.
2422 6th St., 205-523-5506
ladyelines.square.site

The Kentuck Gallery at Hotel Indigo
Open during Hotel Indigo regular hours and from 6 to 7:30 p.m. during First Friday Art Walk.
111 Greensboro Ave., 205-758-1257
kentuck.org

The Paul R. Jones Museum
An essential part of the education and development of UA students and the community. First Friday of each month hours are 5 to 7 p.m.
2308 6th St., 205-345-3038
paulrjonescollection.as.ua.edu

TOUR A LANDMARK IN CIVIL RIGHTS HISTORY
AT FOSTER AUDITORIUM

Built in 1939 and renovated in 2009, Foster Auditorium has been a past location for Alabama basketball and women's sports, plus gatherings such as graduations, lectures, and concerts. Important in the history of the Civil Rights Movement, Foster Auditorium, named for former UA president Richard Clarke Foster, was the scene of the "Stand in the Schoolhouse Door" incident. Alabama Governor George C. Wallace stood in the building doorway on registration day (June 11, 1963), attempting to block two Black students from enrolling at UA. President John F. Kennedy called out the Alabama National Guard to facilitate the situation and Wallace reluctantly stepped aside. This event will forever be recognized as a turning point in Alabama Civil Rights History. Today, Foster Auditorium continues to house sporting and other events including UA volleyball.

801 6th Ave., 205-348-5666
rolltide.com/sports/2016/6/10/facilities-fosterauditorium-html.aspx

ADDITIONAL HISTORIC SITES NOT TO MISS

Battle-Friedman House
1010 Greensboro Ave., 205-758-2238
historictuscaloosa.org/the-battle-friedman-house

First African Baptist Church
2621 Stillman Blvd., 205-758-2833
firstafricanchurch.org

Gorgas House Museum
The oldest structure on the UA campus.
810 Capstone Dr., 205-348-5906
gorgashouse.museums.ua.edu

Jemison-Van de Graaff Mansion
1305 Greensboro Ave., 205-758-2238
jemisonmansion.com

Murphy-Collins House & Murphy African-American Museum
2601 Paul W. Bryant Dr., 205-758-2861
historictuscaloosa.org/the-murphy-collins-house

GET A GLIMPSE OF EARLY TUSCALOOSA ARCHITECTURE
AT THE OLD TAVERN MUSEUM

Architecture enthusiasts and history buffs alike live to tour a relic like the Old Tavern, a staple of Tuscaloosa's landscape since 1827. Built by William Dunton, a local hotelkeeper, the Tavern has served as a tavern, of course, a stagecoach inn, and a residence to many. With three bedrooms upstairs and three downstairs, the asymmetrical layout of the building, along with an exterior chimney breast, and an overhanging balcony gives strong French vibes. Acquired by deed in the mid-1960s, the Tuscaloosa County Preservation Society moved the tavern to its current home at Capitol Park and began a restoration of the facility. Current-day visitors will see the historic structure as a museum recounting the early history of Tuscaloosa County. Tours are available Tuesday through Saturday at 1:30 p.m. and virtually on their website.

500 Nicks Kids Ave., 205-758-2238
historictuscaloosa.org/the-old-tavern

FUN FACT
William Dunton also managed the Golden Ball Hotel back in the day. Today, DePalma's Italian Cafe resides in that location.

LEARN LOCAL HISTORY FROM A SELF-GUIDED WALKING TOUR
OF THE TUSCALOOSA CIVIL RIGHTS TRAIL

Learn the stories of Tuscaloosa's local civil rights movement through a carefully curated, 18-stop downtown walking tour. Stroll at your own pace, and use the handy map and informational guide on their website to gather thoughts and emotions associated with each stop. Opened in June of 2019, the Tuscaloosa Civil Rights Trail documents stories like the enslaved people auctioned before the Civil War, local lynchings, segregation, and many other tragic events that shaped the course of history as the city fought to break the color barrier. Well done and highly educational, the trail stands for a purpose—honoring the stories of the foot soldiers during the Tuscaloosa Civil Rights Movement. Stops along the trail include Capitol Park, the old jail, Paul R. Jones Museum, Murphy-Collins House, Howard-Linton Barbershop, several churches, and other significant places of importance during the Tuscaloosa Civil Rights Movement.

civilrightstuscaloosa.org/civil-rights-trail
facebook.com/tuscaloosacivilrightstrail

BROADEN YOUR KNOWLEDGE
AT MILDRED WESTERVELT WARNER TRANSPORTATION MUSEUM

Another gem along the Black Warrior River, the Mildred Westervelt Warner Transportation Museum makes its home in Queen City Park, more specifically in the Queen City Pool House. Constructed in 1943 for use by Tuscaloosa residents, this site included a poured concrete bathhouse, wading pool, and an Art Deco fountain. Funding for the facility was made possible through the David Warner Foundation, established by the Warner family following the tragic loss of their son David in a drowning accident. The pool house was vacant from the late 1980s until 2005 when it was transformed into a local history museum using a grant from the Alabama Department of Transportation. The pool was filled in during renovation and on December 13, 2011, the former bath house reopened as the Mildred Westervelt Warner Transportation Museum, a place to trace the city's history following transportation system developments.

1901 Jack Warner Pkwy., 205-248-4931
warnertransportationmuseum@ua.edu

FUN FACT

Don Buel Schuyler, the architect who built the original pool house, was an apprentice under famed architect Frank Lloyd Wright. Today, the building is on the National Register of Historic Places, and the museum is owned by the City of Tuscaloosa with daily operations managed by the University of Alabama Museums.

ADDITIONAL HISTORIC SITES NOT TO MISS

Battle-Friedman House
1010 Greensboro Ave., 205-758-2238
historictuscaloosa.org/the-battle-friedman-house

Capitol Park
2828 6th St., 205-562-3210

First African Baptist Church
2621 Stillman Blvd., 205-758-2833
firstafricanchurch.org

Gorgas House Museum
The oldest structure on the UA campus.
810 Capstone Dr., 205-348-5906
gorgashouse.museums.ua.edu

Jemison-Van de Graaff Mansion
1305 Greensboro Ave., 205-758-2238
jemisonmansion.com

Murphy-Collins House & Murphy African-American Museum
2601 Paul W. Bryant Dr., 205-758-2861
historictuscaloosa.org/the-murphy-collins-house

SUPPORT THE MISSION
OF KENTUCK ART CENTER AND FESTIVAL

Kentuck Art Center offers programming that includes cost-free opportunities for emerging artists to indulge in art and culture seven days a week. An important and integral service that lends a hand to underserved communities, Kentuck sticks to their guns when it comes to providing these programs, and they are continually searching for ways to expand their reach. The Kentuck Festival of the Arts, an annual two-day event each October, is the most revenue-producing drive of the year for the center. It is well attended and creates a sizzling $5.5 million in community economic impact. The award-winning festival has roots in folk art and showcases well over 250 artists, live music, craft demonstrations, food trucks, local craft brews, and activities for children. If you are in town and can't make it over to nearby Northport, consider visiting the Kentuck Gallery at Tuscaloosa's Hotel Indigo.

503 Main Ave., Northport, 205-758-1257
kentuck.org

TAKE A GANDER
AT THE UNIVERSITY OF ALABAMA PRESIDENT'S MANSION

Anyone who appreciates architecture will certainly appreciate the University of Alabama President's Mansion. Situated on the UA campus along University Boulevard, the historic Greek Revival–style mansion cannot be missed and is a great place to snap a souvenir selfie. The official housing for university presidents since completion in 1841, the mansion continues this tradition still today, in addition to utilizing this beautiful setting for executive photo shoots for groups and organizations associated with the university. The American Civil War almost brought destruction to the mansion, but escaping harm allowed it to become one of the oldest surviving buildings on UA's present-day campus. Having equal parts historical and architectural importance, the President's Mansion earned a spot on the National Register of Historic Places and was officially added on January 14, 1972.

717 University Blvd., 205-348-5666
calendar.ua.edu/presidents_mansion_108

ABSORB THE HERITAGE SITE HISTORY
AT MOUNDVILLE ARCHAEOLOGICAL PARK

The University of Alabama's Moundville Archaeological Park is one of the country's leading Native American heritage sites with occupancy noted between AD 1000 and AD 1450. When population was at its largest, the Moundville community settled in a 300-acre village overlooking the Black Warrior River and was labeled by *National Geographic* as "The Big Apple of the 14th Century." Today, the park is a preservation of this acreage where the Mississippian people built giant, flat-top, earthen mounds. Arranged surrounding a central plaza, the mounds served multiple purposes including residences, mortuaries, and religious centers. About AD 1350, Moundville began to decline and by the 1500s was mostly abandoned, baffling scholars to this day. Present-day visitors enjoy views of the monuments as well as the river, a short nature trail, campground, picnic areas, and a park museum where the famous stone Rattlesnake Disk is on display. Don't skip the lovely Knotted Bird Gifts gift shop.

634 Mound State Pkwy., Moundville, 205-371-2234
moundville.museums.ua.edu

TIP

Come in October for the annual Moundville Native American Festival. See the work of artisans, performers, and demonstrators who keep cultural knowledge alive through this annual event. Visit the website for yearly specific dates and read through the simple, yet important, etiquette considerations.

moundville.museums.ua.edu

REFLECT ON HISTORY
AT VETERANS MEMORIAL PARK

A one-acre plot set aside for a purpose, Veterans Memorial Park serves as a memorial for United States Armed Forces veterans on the site of former Northington General Army Hospital. Northington was a large military hospital and as it closed at the end of World War II, stipulations were made that this acre would serve as a shrine, a memorial to veterans, or a denominational church. Today, visitors can walk the grounds and see remnants of the USS *Tuscaloosa* CA-37 battle cruiser, a suspended Vought A-7E Corsair, and other military machinery. Also, notice the engraved monuments scattered around the park bearing names of veterans—gone, but not forgotten. Memorial Day and Veterans Day are special times at the park and offer events to celebrate and remember those who lost their lives in service with the US Armed Forces. Check the website for more information on these events.

1701 McFarland Blvd. E, 205-562-3220
tcpara.org/parks/veterans-memorial-park

REMEMBER TUSCALOOSA AS A PREVIOUS STATE CAPITOL
AT CAPITOL PARK

Many people recognize Tuscaloosa as "Title Town" in celebration of athletic accolades. But, long before that, this West Alabama town had a different title bearing remarkable significance to the history of Alabama. In 1826, the Alabama State Capitol site moved from Cahaba to Tuscaloosa where it remained until 1846. William Nichols was the designer given the nod for the capitol building project where he showcased a beautiful display of Greek Revival and Federal styles of architecture. When the baton was passed and Montgomery became the new state capitol location, the building was used for the Alabama Central Female College. A fire destroyed the school/old capitol building in August of 1923. Today the remains, including the stone foundation and a couple of small columns, serve as reminders of Tuscaloosa's important past and focal points of Capitol Park. Easily accessible in the downtown area, Capitol Park is a lovely place for reflection.

2828 6th St., 205-562-3210
visittuscaloosa.com/listing/capitol-park

ROAM THE GROUNDS
OF GREENWOOD CEMETERY

For those who love wandering through cemeteries, don't sleep on this one. Greenwood is Tuscaloosa's oldest cemetery situated in close proximity to the downtown area. Past the iron gate, you'll find a 200-year-old cemetery with many beautiful headstones (some are marble and were carved in New Orleans) and a relatively quiet atmosphere. Notable locals who were significant in Tuscaloosa's history have been laid to rest here. You'll also notice several family plots, some of which have their own gates surrounding the perimeter. It won't take long to find yourself completely immersed in reading headstones and gazing at sculptures. It's a special place to residents, but often visitors fall in love with Greenwood Cemetery, too. From trees that date back to the early 1820s to monuments paying tribute to folks of yesteryear, this cemetery holds much history for Tuscaloosa.

Intersection of 29th Ave. and 11th St.

ADD SUSPENSE TO YOUR TRIP
WITH HAUNTED TUSCALOOSA TOURS

Sometimes history and haunts go hand-in-hand. If you are a fan of paranormal adventures, consider Haunted Tuscaloosa Tours presented by the Friends of Drish. You'll visit 16 locations in this hour-and-a-half jaunt. Places like the Drish House, the Jemison-Van de Graaff Mansion, and others will offer a splash of Tuscaloosa history with a haunting amount of speculation. You'll hear the tale of the Drish House where Dr. John R. Drish fell to his death from the top of the stairwell in 1867 amid rumors of gambling and drinking. His wife, Sarah, is said to haunt the house even today. Also, look for the Jemison-Van de Graaff Mansion, a spacious Italianate mansion boasting more than 20 rooms. Riddled with a storied past including suicide and depression, Tuscaloosa's most haunted home has reports of ghosts wandering hallways and other unexplainable haunted happenings. Put this on your list . . . if you dare.

visittuscaloosa.com/haunted-places-in-tuscaloosa

TIP
Haunted Tuscaloosa Tours are only active during the month of October. Children under 8 years old are not permitted and under 12 years old must be accompanied by an adult. To purchase tickets, go to visittuscaloosa.com/haunted-places-in-tuscaloosa.

DRIVE ON OVER
TO THE MERCEDES-BENZ VISITOR CENTER

Many people traveling to Tuscaloosa don't realize that the only Mercedes-Benz museum, short of a trip to Germany, is located here. And, it makes perfect sense with the luxury automaker manufacturing several of its most popular vehicles in Tuscaloosa County for more than 20 years. Open since the late 1990s, the recently renovated visitor center is a haven of exhibits and concepts that share the story of history and culture for an amazing German automotive brand. Expect an interactive tour highlighting innovative, iconic Mercedes-Benz products including the 1886 Benz Patented Motor Car, race cars, and more. Divided into five distinct areas (innovation, performance, safety, vision, and design), the visitor center aptly showcases Mercedes-Benz, yesterday and today. Visitors are welcome Monday through Friday and admission is free. Be sure and stop at the gift shop for fun souvenirs.

6 Mercedes Dr., Vance, 205-507-2252
mbusi.com/visitorcenter

TIP
If a factory tour is on your must-do list, you must reserve it in advance by calling 205-507-2252.

114

DISCOVER THE HISTORY OF A NEARBY COMMUNITY
AT NORTHPORT HERITAGE MUSEUM

For the many history buffs out there who go out of their way to visit a local museum, you'll find value in the Northport Heritage Museum. Part of Tuscaloosa County, Northport is a small community that shares much of the same history as the college town, yet some of its very own. Located next to the community center near downtown Northport, you'll notice the 1907 Victorian-era home as you pull in. So pretty, and an unexpectedly charming space for a museum. Spend some time wandering through exhibits and examining photographs depicting Northport's history beginning as a Native American settlement back in 1816. Special exhibits are the A.H. Bean World Photographic Collection and the Peterson Military Uniform Collection. If you'd like to have a group tour of the museum, please call ahead.

1991 Park St., Northport, 205-339-8891
tourwestalabama.com/attraction/northport-heritage-museum

SHOPPING
AND FASHION

SHOP FOR OFFICIALLY LICENSED UA GEAR
AT THE SUPE STORE

From course materials and supplies to technology and the latest in MacBooks and Apple Watches, UA students can find every tool needed for success in the classroom. But, there's another element to the University of Alabama Supply Store aka the Supe Store. Students, faculty, fans, and visitors flock to the popular store for all the latest in Bama merch! With two locations, the Supe Store offers officially licensed basics like T-shirts, caps, and hoodies along with UA Nike apparel like polos, jerseys, shorts, hats, and shoes. There's an exclusive line of lululemon clothing and accessories in addition to Yeti and Tervis items, all emblazoned with the Alabama logo. Gifts and souvenirs, purses, Gameday Boots, kids toys, and all the buttons and pins your heart desires are available in-store and online (they ship!).

University of Alabama Supply Store Student Center
Located in the Undergraduate Admissions Welcome Center
751 Campus W Dr., 205-348-6168

The Corner Supe Store
807 Paul W Bryant Dr., 205-348-9724
universitysupplystore.com

TIP

A beautiful bonus to shopping with the Supe Store is that your purchases fund scholarships and other University of Alabama campus programs. Now that's winning!

BUY TRENDY GAME-DAY APPAREL
AT PANTS STORE TUSCALOOSA

Looking for fashion-forward choices in athleisure, dressy boutique pieces, upscale shoe brands, game-day must-haves, and accessories? Pants Store is likely your kind of place! With a broad selection of clothing and accessories for men, women, boys, and girls, dressing for the big game, work, casual outings, or a night out is easy, affordable, and fun. Founded in 1950 by pant jobber Taylor Gee, people shopping from his Leeds warehouse bins filled with pants quickly dubbed it "The Pants Store." Today, grandsons of Gee continue to operate six locations of the retail boutique-like stores scattered from Birmingham to Tuscaloosa, Auburn, and Huntsville. Present-day Pants Store Tuscaloosa carries far more than pants, and showcases dozens upon dozens of popular brands, but also continues to put customers first. That speaks volumes.

2223 University Blvd., 205-210-4012
pantsstore.com

PREPARE FOR
THE GREAT OUTDOORS
AT WOODS & WATER

For more than 35 years, Woods & Water has been the go-to store for hunters and fishermen in search of equipment, supplies, apparel (including camo), backpacks, wallets, gifts, and so much more. Locally owned and operated, Woods & Water caters to outdoor enthusiasts with well-known brands such as Arc'teryx, Columbia, Marmot, the North Face, Patagonia, Vasque, Frye, and a host of others. Additionally, the outdoor retail store is the largest dealer of Yeti and Costa in the Southeast. The experience of shopping at Woods & Water is one of fun and appreciation for finding everything you need under one roof. Deer stands and duck blinds? They've got 'em! Archery equipment? It's the place! Coolers and sleeping bags? You bet! They also carry weather radios, and if you're from the South, you know how important that is. Woods & Water is a Tuscaloosa treasure that you'll thoroughly enjoy visiting.

5101 Summit Ridge, 205-342-4868
woods-n-water.com

PICK OUT
CLOSET FAVORITES
AT THE SHIRT SHOP

When your wardrobe calls for something a little extra, consider the Shirt Shop where the finest brands yield exceptional choices. Game-day attire is turned up a notch with men's Peter Millar designer pieces (think upscale polos and outerwear) and women's selections from Ellsworth & Ivey like gorgeous sweaters and T-shirts. Feeling fancy? The Shirt Shop offers tailored clothing (dress shirts and pants) along with accessories like cuff links, bow ties, pocket squares, belts, and Johnston & Murphy shoes. Gift giving has never been so easy for the Tide fan on your shopping list with the Shirt Shop's selection of specialty clothing items such as the T-Town Polo or the Bryant Polo. Show up in style with legendary Alabama fanfare wardrobe pieces you'll find readily available in Downtown T-Town at the Shirt Shop.

525 Greensboro Ave., 205-752-6931
theshirtshop.biz

THRIFT DESIGNER CLOTHES AND ACCESSORIES
AT TWICE AS NICE CONSIGNMENT SHOP

Today's culture of repurposing and reusing definitely includes thrifting and consigning as a shopping means for many pocketbooks. An almost 40-year-old business and treasure in Tuscaloosa's downtown community, Twice as Nice Consignment Shop has evolved from a children's-only consignment store to a full-fledged conglomerate adding adult clothing (mainly designer and boutique brands), shoes, designer bags, accessories, jewelry, artwork, books, instruments, furniture, and seasonal merchandise. Frugal and savvy shoppers come in daily to scour through pre-owned items that often can be purchased new with tags for a fraction of the original price. Sometimes people just don't realize the value of what they're consigning and that's a big win for shoppers looking for that special item undervalued by others. Who doesn't love a bargain, and this is the place to find one!

2319 University Blvd., 205-758-6343
facebook.com/twiceasnicebama

ELEVATE YOUR WARDROBE
AT THE LOCKER ROOM

Since 1964, the Locker Room has been offering the finest in men's apparel from dress and casual wear to University of Alabama licensed merchandise (clothing, shoes, and accessories). Brands are important, and here you'll find those that resonate with high quality like Johnnie-O, Peter Millar, David Donahue, Holderness & Bourne, Smathers & Branson, and more. The Locker Room is where guys come to find an official crimson blazer made from 100 percent worsted wool with houndstooth lining and UA crest buttons, a Dixieland Delight T-shirt, and a full line of ElephantWear shirts and hats. To complete the look, don't forget to browse the footwear on hand from Martin Dingman and Smathers & Branson—high dollar, snazzy, and sure to make you feel like a million bucks! Shop in-store or online, and always be the most dapper version of yourself.

2104 University Blvd., 205-752-2990
locker-room.biz

RACK UP ON PERFECT SOUVENIRS
AT ALABAMA EXPRESS

Have you ever seen a "RAMMER JAMMER" or "BEAT (fill in the blank)" game-day button and wondered where it came from? Alabama Express could be the place! With an impressive myriad of buttons, decals, wooden plaques, toys, giftware, clothing (including babies and toddlers), hats, and other miscellaneous items, University of Alabama sports fans can always find something exciting that they didn't know they needed. It's always fun to see the types of items visitors pick up for souvenirs as well. Pet toys and collars, ornaments, football earrings, fleece blankets, and officially licensed Alabama oversized umbrellas and hoodies. Find your "Alabama Mom" magnet or car decal, pachyderm socks, and loads of other random goodies at Alabama Express, located right on the main strip. You can browse online or visit in person.

1141 University Blvd., 205-391-2095
alabama.express

TIP
Those cute toddler-size University of Alabama cheerleader uniforms? This is a great place to pick them up!

SEARCH FOR ANTIQUES
AT OLIVE TREE

For some folks, the search for antiques and treasures is all about the thrill of the hunt. For others, it's a way of life. No matter which category you fall into, don't overlook a trip to Tuscaloosa for an exciting opportunity to go antique scavenging. Start your search for home furnishings, decor, and other gems at Olive Tree, a local antique store with furniture, home accessories, and garden items. Owner Chris Roycroft has quite a collection to sift through as Olive Tree has been around for some 20 years and likely has something on your wish list or something you didn't know you needed. Take your time searching through the plethora of items for sale at Olive Tree. Look carefully at the craftsmanship, and before you know it, you will have a keen idea about the kinds of pieces you desire for your own home collection. Happy hunting!

2228 University Blvd., 205-758-7424
facebook.com/olivetreeantiques

UNCOVER A COLLECTIBLE
AT ALABAMA VINTAGE

Alabama Vintage is the cutest little shop brimming with collectibles, vintage clothing (T-shirts, outerwear, jerseys, and hats in many university sports), non-Alabama merchandise, and occasionally some new items as well. You never know what you're going to find, but it's always good-quality throwbacks that many Roll Tide fans have tucked away in their memories. Popular items folks seem to be on the hunt for include sweatshirts, varsity jackets, windbreakers, buttons, age-old jerseys, and even a selection of player and team-issued gear often with the tags still attached. Don't overlook this unique storefront in downtown Tuscaloosa for additional hats and shirts from other sports teams, both college and professional. Shop in-store or online, and grab a gift card for someone special who may also appreciate the opportunity to look for a collectible of their liking.

2210 University Blvd., 205-248-7261
alabamavtg.com

TIP
Due to the nature of merchandise at Alabama Vintage, you'll find items turn over quickly. It's best to check the website and social media accounts often to keep tabs on current offerings.
Facebook: @AlabamaVTG
Instagram: @alabamavtg

FIND A RARE TITLE
AT ERNEST & HADLEY BOOKSELLERS

Looking for a unique selection of new and used books, or perhaps a rare title? Allow some time to step into Ernest & Hadley Booksellers for these and other creative materials sourced locally, regionally, and internationally for a diverse range of reading materials. The store offers a community space for book clubs to meet, book signings, and artist exhibits. Check the online schedule for upcoming events of interest.

Maybe you're wondering about the name. During a trip to Paris, the future indie bookstore owners stumbled upon the Latin Quarter apartment once occupied by Ernest Hemingway and his first wife, Hadley. A sign above the door referenced this location as "the happiest time in their marriage." Turns out that Ernest & Hadley was a fitting name for this Tuscaloosa bookstore, recognized by its owners as their happy place.

1928 7th St., 205-632-5331
ernestandhadleybooks.com

SCOUR THE FARMERS MARKET
AT TUSCALOOSA RIVER MARKET

Beautifully situated on the banks of the Black Warrior River, the River Market plays host to many spectacular Tuscaloosa events from weddings, fundraisers, and other special gatherings to the weekly farmers market. Get your weekend going in the right direction with a trip to the Saturday farmers market (open from 7 a.m. to noon), held year-round with a slew of fantastic vendors each week. It's a place to bring family and friends, meander the booths while sipping coffee, and knock some things off your shopping list. With 70 or more vendors, you'll find a bounty of local crops that includes fruits, vegetables, and grass-fed meat. Also, browse all the booths to find delicious homemade treats and unique artisans. Finish your morning with a River Walk stroll for extra relaxation.

1900 Jack Warner Pkwy., 205-248-5295
tuscaloosafarmersmarket.com

TIP
If you are looking for certain vendors or just want to see who will be there each Saturday, check out the website or Instagram account for frequent updates.
tuscaloosafarmersmarket.com/meet-our-vendors
Instagram: @tuscaloosarivermarket

SHOP 'TIL YOU DROP
AT MIDTOWN VILLAGE

If you love lots of shopping in one place, head over to Midtown Village in the heart of Tuscaloosa on McFarland Boulevard. Great dining opportunities are strewn throughout the complex as well as upscale boutiques, Barnes & Noble, Best Buy, health and beauty-related shops (think lash spa, massages, nails, and hair salons), shoe stores, and other fashion stores (J. Jill, Chico's, Loft, White House/Black Market, and others). A Crawford Square property, common areas are neat, clean, and create a safe feeling while shopping. Follow online for property functions like outdoor movies, special events (Harvest Jam is in October each year), workshops, fashion shows…even a Puppy Palooza! Restaurant Happy Hour details are sometimes posted on the site as well. Shop, have a massage, grab a book or gift, and have a fantastic meal without even moving your vehicle. Everyone can get onboard with that.

1800 McFarland Blvd. E, 866-644-2521
midtownvillagetuscaloosa.com

CURATE YOUR CLOSET
AT SPARROW MARKETPLACE

In search of a new outfit for the weekend game or something fun to add to your travel wardrobe on a weekend trip? Sparrow Marketplace might be the answer! Shopping is a pleasure at this women's boutique, minority owned and female run, offering a wide variety of clothes, shoes, and accessories. Browse favorite brands like Billini and Steve Madden for quality pieces that will enhance your look, and showcase your very own personality with accessories from trendy bags to fabulous jewelry. Many shoppers visit Sparrow for inspiration in updating their personal closet while others simply want the latest fashion piece to stand out in a crowd. Sparrow's online fashion blog shares great tips along with the most current fashion news and upcoming launches so you can stay in the loop. Shop at the brick-and-mortar boutique or online.

1800 McFarland Blvd. E, Ste. 114B, 205-737-7449
sparrowmarketplace.com

TIP
Read Sparrow Marketplace's blog online at sparrowmarketplace.com/blogs/news and let their team encourage your closet curations with fabulous styling tips.

SMELL AMAZING
WITH PRODUCTS FROM
BUFF CITY SOAP

Buff City Soap has a Soap Makery in the Tuscaloosa market located in Midtown Village. Known for handmade soaps, skin care, bath, laundry, and other household products, Buff City uses only plant-based ingredients that are paraben and phthalate free. Shoppers have the opportunity to choose a product (bar soap, bath bomb, hand soap, laundry soap, etc.) in the scent of their choice from about 30 fragrance options. The best part is that everything is created in the Soap Makery from mixing and pouring to cutting and packaging, so it's fresh as can be. Great for gift giving and for yourself. Gather your friends, family, even coworkers, and schedule a bath bomb party! Make delightfully scented bath bombs while celebrating a birthday, team building, or any occasion. No harsh ingredients, lots of scents and products to choose from—check out Buff City Soap during your visit to T-Town.

1800 McFarland Blvd. E, 205-737-7089
Instagram: @buffcitysoap.tuscaloosa

ADD SOMETHING SPECIAL TO YOUR HOME
FROM LOU & COMPANY

Tuscaloosa has a hidden gem and it's named after a goldendoodle, Lou. Sydney Burns opened the sweetest, most chic gift store in town with the help of her mom, Kelli, back in 2016. A University of Alabama alumna, Sydney quickly curated a mix of upscale home goods and fabulous gift products that wowed shoppers. Amassing a loyal following of shoppers who adored her taste, Sydney soon needed more room. Today, the setting of Lou & Company's storefront is lavish and inviting, with space for browsers to notice one-of-a-kind items that are destined to make perfect gifts. Specialty items are hand-chosen by Sydney and often are locally sourced. You'll find the latest in high-end seasonal gifts and products ranging from art, pillows, and bedding to custom stationery, partyware, accessories, even baby items. Pop in for a specific purpose or just to ooo and ah. Both are acceptable.

1922 University Blvd., Ste. A, 205-872-8050
shoplouandco.com

BUILD A GIFT BASKET
AT BRADLEY'S MARKET

Talk about one-stop shopping—Bradley's Market is incredible! A University of Alabama graduate in clinical nutrition, Bradley Bailey turned her love for food, cooking, and entertaining into a shopping and market experience that would fill a need in the Tuscaloosa community. Patterning the market after her aunt's successful concept in Atlanta, Bradley compiled the perfect mix of prepared foods along with flowers, produce, specialty items, and gifts in a setting where customers could multitask with ease. Build a gift basket and surprise someone special with a uniquely selected grouping of items just for them. Choose pieces for your home that revolve around your personality from linens, place mats, barware, dinnerware, and stemware to books, vases, frames, seasonal merchandise, and must-have tailgate necessities. Need a unique gift? An elephant bottle stopper or vintage wine glasses should do just fine. And don't skip on the specialty foods section . . . that's where the real jewels are.

700 Towncenter Blvd., 205-764-1939
bradleysmarket.com

FURNISH YOUR HOME OR BUY AN INSPIRATIONAL GIFT
AT EVERLASTING GIFTS & HOME STORE

Everlasting Gifts and their Home Store are only a block apart in Historic Downtown Northport just across the river from downtown Tuscaloosa. A family-owned business backed with loads of charm, and beautiful, inspirational gifts, in addition to a Home Store with timeless furniture, lamps, rugs, and artwork, combine for the best in an interior/home decor shopping experience. The quality of furniture is exceptional with dining tables and chairs, buffets, bedside tables, chests, and gorgeous accent chairs among the selections. Also, take a peek at the chandeliers and large wall art . . . you might find something just perfect to take back home and complete a room. A visit to the gift shop is worth your time as there are so many great items for sale. You'll see artisan jewelry, candles, local honey, pottery, and other unique treasures that you'll want to purchase as extra special remembrances of your time in West Alabama.

433 Main Ave., Northport, 205-872-8864
everlastinginspiredliving.com

MUST-STOP SHOPS FOR THE TIDE FAN
IN THE TUSCALOOSA AREA

These three retail establishments are paramount to a Tuscaloosa visit. Fun, fashion-forward, and filled with lots of love for the University of Alabama—don't sleep on these shops.

Alumni Hall
This store offers great brands and affordable prices on UA apparel, gifts, and merchandise. Things you can find here include Nike official sideline clothing, women's accessories, and a selection for kids.
Show your military ID for 10 percent off.
Midtown Village, 1800 McFarland Blvd. E, Ste. 504, 205-523-7562
alumnihall.com/alabama-crimson-tide

Bama Fever
An oldie but goodie, this store has Crimson Tide clothing, merchandise for the car and home, buttons, key chains, and more.
The Shoppes at Legacy Park, 1320 McFarland Blvd. E, 205-632-3370
shopbamafever.com

High Tide Sports
A family-owned business specializing in gifts, accessories, and clothing (tees, spirit jerseys, and more).
University Mall, 1701 McFarland Blvd. E, 205-554-7596

ACTIVITIES
BY SEASON

FALL

WINTER

SUGGESTED
ITINERARIES

HISTORY BUFFS

COUPLES' LONG WEEKEND

• •

• •

FAMILY-FRIENDLY FUN

INDEX